BURNOUT

BURNOUT

MYRON RUSH

VICTOR BOOKS™

A DIVISION OF SCRIPTURE PRESS PUBLICATIONS INC.
USA CANADA ENGLAND

Scripture quotations marked NIV are from the *Holy Bible, New International Version,* © 1973, 1978, 1984, International Bible Society. Used by permission of Zondervan Bible Publishers. Verses marked TLB are taken from *The Living Bible,* © 1971, Tyndale House Publishers, Wheaton, IL 60189. Used by permission. Verses marked RSV are from the *Revised Standard Version of the Bible,* © 1946, 1952, 1971, 1973. Verses marked KJV are from the *King James Version.*

Recommended Dewey Decimal Classification: 158.6
Suggested Subject Heading: APPLIED PSYCHOLOGY

Library of Congress Catalog Card Number: 86-63105
ISBN: 0-89693-242-7

CONTENTS

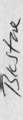

This book is dedicated to
JIM ANDER
my very dear friend
and former business partner,
who faithfully stood by me,
encouraged me,
believed in me,
and helped me recover
from the depths of burnout.

I walked into the apartment, tossed my coat over the back of a chair, and turned and locked the door behind me. On my way to the living room I took the phone off the hook. And after pulling the drapes closed, I slumped down in an overstuffed chair and closed my eyes.

When you burn both ends of the candle as long as I had, eventually the flame goes out. My life seemed pitch-dark. I was mentally, emotionally, physically, and spiritually exhausted.

My unbalanced life of too much work and not enough play had created some business success but enormous problems at home. After twenty-three years of marriage I suddenly found myself alone in a small, dumpy, two-bedroom apartment.

In addition to my full-time consulting business, I had in the past three years helped start two new companies. One was a manufacturing business; the other, a marketing and sales organization.

When we started the manufacturing company, I spent 100 of the last 120 days of that year living out of a suitcase. During that period I traveled across eleven states interviewing potential dealers 6 days (and nights) a week.

In my spare time that year I managed to write two books, conduct numerous management seminars around the country, teach two elective Sunday School classes at church, and start a home Bible study with a group of couples in our neighborhood.

In two years our two companies had gone from an idea in our minds to an operation with over fifty employees. We moved two times in one year because of rapid growth. The faster we grew, the more people we needed to hire, and the more problems we had to solve. My original excitement, enthusiasm, and high energy level slowly turned into frustration, resentment, and fatigue. And now three years later I had just signed an agreement to sell my interest in our two companies to my partners.

I was shocked by my feelings. I had always been a very positive, highly motivated, achievement-oriented person. And there I sat, alone in a dark apartment, not caring whether I ever walked out the front door again. My confidence in myself was gone. My goals had vanished. The love and concern I had once had for people had turned into dislike and resentment. And most shocking of all, my once-strong love for God had turned into apathy.

I opened my eyes, got up from the overstuffed chair, and slowly walked around the apartment, finally winding up in the bathroom. As I stared at myself in the mirror I thought, *Where has the Myron I knew gone?* All I saw was the empty shell he had left behind when he moved out—I was truly burned out!

The following pages of this book deal with burnout—its causes, its symptoms, its results, how to overcome it, and most important, how to avoid it.

As a management consultant and businessman I have dealt with burnout in my clients, my employees, and myself. I have counseled people who were burned out, and I have been counseled for burnout. I can speak from experience that with God's help it is possible to escape from the clutches of burnout and climb to new heights in life. And not only is it possible to overcome burnout, but the experience can help you become a better person.

ONE

BURNOUT: MAKING SPECTATORS OUT OF HIGH ACHIEVERS

When you burn both ends of a candle, it may produce twice as much light, but the candle burns out twice as fast. That is a good analogy for the burnout process. People experiencing burnout suddenly discover that all of their mental, emotional, and physical energies have been consumed. They have exhausted their strength and lost their will to persevere.

Burnout can be defined as *the type of stress and emotional fatigue, frustration, and exhaustion that occurs when a series of (or combination of) events in a relationship, mission, way of life, or job fail to produce an expected result*. Burnout usually occurs to goal-oriented high achievers who are driven to succeed. Their appointment books are usually full, and they have always done more than their share of the work.

Burnout is not a respecter of persons. It occurs in people of all walks of life. Doctors, teachers, bus drivers, counselors, pastors, homemakers, students—all can experience burnout syndrome. Burnout occurs in young and old alike. Social and financial status have no bearing on the probability of becoming burned out.

Most people experiencing burnout do not have a history of emotional or mental disturbances. They are neither neurotic nor psychotic as we would medically define those terms. But all

13

people suffering from burnout are hurting emotionally and psychologically—and usually spiritually.

THE HIGH COST OF BURNOUT

One of the greatest tragedies of burnout is that it strikes our most productive people. Because burnout tends to strike high-achievement, goal-oriented people, not only is the personal loss great, but the loss to organizations and businesses can be devastating. For example, Wayne Gardner had been the pastor of Hillside Community Church for sixteen years. He was only the second pastor the church had ever had. When Wayne became pastor at Hillside, the average attendance for the Sunday morning worship service was about fifty people. Wayne had a real heart for people, and he also had the rare combination of gifts of being both an excellent pastor-teacher and a fine administrator.

The church began to grow under Wayne's leadership, and within three years they were in their first building program. During the next ten years the church started a school (grades K–12) and went through two more building programs. The church started a local radio ministry and then a television ministry. In addition to his other gifts, Wayne was an excellent counselor, and his services were in great demand in the community.

However, as the church continued to grow, so did Wayne's responsibilities. His desire to serve people made it difficult to say no to any need. As a result he slowly overextended himself. The demands people made on his time began to cut into the time he usually set aside for study and sermon preparation. He began spending more and more late-night hours in his study at home trying to get caught up.

Slowly Wayne became both emotionally and physically exhausted, but his commitment to the ministry and the high standard of excellence he demanded from himself caused him to work even harder to try to stay on top of his duties and fulfill what he considered to be his God-given obligations to the people of the church and local community. Unfortunately, this only added to Wayne's frustration and fatigue. One day he realized he was starting to resent it when people asked for counseling appointments. In fact, he resented every "interruption."

He began to feel guilty for his negative feelings toward people and became even more frustrated with his work and himself. Finally he started questioning whether he was fit to be a pastor. Eventually he decided to leave the ministry. The church board was shocked when Wayne turned in his resignation.

After Wayne left, the church no longer had the benefit of his strong leadership, and people began to leave the church. Eventually the church had to eliminate many of the programs and activities that had allowed it to have an effective outreach in the community.

Wayne Gardner is a vivid example of the high cost of burnout to both individuals and organizations. However, the large majority of people experiencing burnout don't physically leave their jobs—but their positions are vacant just the same. They go through the motions of making their daily appearances, but they have mentally and emotionally resigned.

WHERE WE'RE GOING

The purpose of this book is to define burnout and identify factors in our society, jobs, and personalities that cause it. We will explore and discuss the symptoms of burnout and their effects on individuals and organizations. Then we will discuss how to overcome burnout. In the last part of the book we will take an in-depth look at ways to avoid burnout syndrome. And finally, we will evaluate the benefits that can be derived and the lessons learned from going through burnout.

Even though burnout is a painful and unpleasant experience, the results can be very beneficial. Burnout is our emotions' way of putting the brakes on and bringing high-achieving, goal-oriented persons to a stop before they self-destruct physically.

In order for our lives to run smoothly, they must be in balance. Burnout is the result of life getting too far out of balance. When the tires on a car get too far out of balance, the car won't steer properly and the tires will wear out very fast. The same is true with our lives. If we get too far out of balance, we are unable to keep our lives on track and we quickly wear out mentally, emotionally, physically, and spiritually. Burnout causes us to bring our activities and daily routines to a halt long enough for us to reevaluate our lives, set new and proper purposes, goals, and priorities, and put balance in our activities in order to become productive people again.

Therefore, if you or someone you know is going through burnout—take heart and be encouraged! It need not be the end of the world. This can be the night before the great new dawn in which you find new meaning, fulfillment, and accomplishments in a new and better day of your life.

A CASE STUDY FROM THE BIBLE

I never cease to be amazed at the Bible's relevance to the day-to-day situations in our lives. I have discovered that the Bible has the answers to all of life's problems. The roadblock is never the Bible's lack of relevance—it is always my lack of obedience.

As a management consultant I have had the opportunity to work with numerous Christian organizations, groups, and individuals over the past several years. I have discovered that burnout is a major problem in the Christian community. In fact, many recent studies indicate that high achievers working in high people-contact and service-oriented jobs are the most prone to burnout. This fits the profile of most Christians—especially Christian leaders.

The Bible makes it clear that past spiritual accomplishments are not necessarily a deterrent to burnout. On the contrary, our past spiritual accomplishments can lead directly to burnout. For an example, let's look at the life of Moses.

The Bible opens the curtain on Moses' adult life in Exodus 2:11-14 by showing us his great love for his own people. His desire to help his people was so strong that he was willing to kill an Egyptian who was beating a Hebrew slave. The next day

Moses tried to settle a fight between two of his own Hebrew people. You might say Moses had a "shepherd's heart" for his people. His love for them was obviously very strong.

In Exodus 4–12 God used Moses to bring the ten plagues against Egypt. Then in chapters 13–14 we find Moses leading the Children of Israel out of Egypt and across the Red Sea. Moses was firmly established as both the spiritual and political leader of the Israelites.

God performed great miracles through Moses. In Exodus 17 the Lord told Moses to strike a rock with his staff; when he did, water came out of the rock for the people and their flocks to drink. Later in the chapter we see Moses serving as commander-in-chief of the Israelite army as they fought and defeated the Amalekites.

Moses' total dedication to the people of Israel is probably best described in Exodus 18. His father-in-law, Jethro, came to visit him.

The next day Moses sat as usual to hear the people's complaints against each other, from morning to evening. When Moses' father-in-law saw how much time this was taking, he said, "Why are you trying to do all this alone, with people standing here all day long to get your help?"

"Well, because the people come to me with their disputes, to ask for God's decisions," Moses told him. "I am their judge, deciding who is right and who is wrong, and instructing them in God's ways. I apply the laws of God to their particular disputes" (Ex. 18:13-16, TLB).

Let's look closely at this scene. Notice that the passage indicates that this scene was an everyday occurrence. Moses was spending all of his time dealing with the people and their problems. Most of his contact with them was to deal with their complaints and disagreements.

However, Moses was not complaining. He matter-of-factly tells Jethro, "I'm just obeying the Lord and doing my job. It's my duty to deal with the people's problems and solve all their disputes" (my paraphrase). Moses certainly displayed a great deal of patience and love for the people in this passage.

Moses continued to serve faithfully as spiritual and political leader of the people. In Exodus 32 we see just how strong Moses' love for the people was. Moses had been up on Mount Sinai to receive the Ten Commandments from God. He was gone longer than the people thought necessary, and they became restless. They talked Aaron, Moses' brother, into building them a golden calf to worship.

When God saw that the people were worshiping an idol, He was furious with them and told Moses, "I have seen what a stubborn, rebellious lot these people are. Now let Me alone and My anger shall blaze out against them and destroy them all; and I will make you, Moses, into a great nation instead of them" (Ex. 32:9-10, TLB).

This would have been a great honor for Moses. He could have become the father of God's chosen people instead of Abraham. But Moses loved these people more than his own life, and he begged God not to do it (vv. 11-13). God listened to Moses and let him continue to lead the people toward the Promised Land.

Moses continued to serve the people. He built the ark of the covenant, the tabernacle, and its furnishings; established the various religious offerings and ceremonies; appointed priests; and established social, medical, and judicial laws. Finally he undertook the enormous job of numbering all the people by clan and tribe.

Moses obviously had great abilities, dearly loved the people, and was a high achiever. But in Numbers 11 Moses is shown to have reached the end of his mental, emotional, and physical ropes—he had burned himself out. He could no longer deal with the people or their problems. All he wanted to do was escape—at any price.

The people had been eating the manna God provided, but they wanted meat to go with it. They went to Moses and complained about the lack of meat in their diet. Moses exploded. Notice what Moses tells God in Numbers 11:11-15.

Moses said to the Lord, "Why pick on me, to give me the burden of a people like this? Are they *my* children? Am I their father? Is that why You have given me the job of nursing them along like babies until we get to the land You promised their ancestors? Where am I supposed to get meat for all these people? . . . I can't carry this nation by myself! The load is far too heavy! If You are going to treat me like this, please kill me right now; it will be a kindness! Let me out of this impossible situation!" (TLB)

Can you believe the change that has occurred in Moses since the golden-calf incident in Exodus 32? Moses was willing to overlook the people's idol worship (which was a violation of one of the Ten Commandments and punishable by death), but now he was ready to have God kill him because the people asked for meat in their diet. What a classic example of burnout syndrome!

This is the same Moses who years earlier had killed an Egyptian for striking a Hebrew. This is the man who was once willing to listen to the people's needs, problems, and complaints all day—day after day—and not complain. But now Moses tells God that the people are too great a burden for him to bear. When the people were in the desert without water for themselves and their flocks, "Moses pleaded with the Lord to help them" (Ex. 15:25, TLB). But now when they are asking for meat, he pleads with God to kill him. We can learn a great deal about the burnout process from Moses' experience.

People helpers are prone to burnout (Ex. 2:11-14). Moses cared deeply about the Hebrew people. Those who care about and are deeply involved with people are more susceptible to burnout than are other people. Studies show that people in such professions as teaching, counseling, social work, health care, law enforcement, and religious work are much more apt to experience burnout than are people working in low people-contact jobs.

High achievers risk burning out (Ex. 18:13-18). High achievers thrive on work. They love a challenge. And they don't know their own limitations. They would rather do the job themselves than take the time to train someone else to do it for them. Moses fit that description.

High achievers tend to overextend themselves, running the risk of emotional and physical exhaustion. This is exactly what Moses did. Notice in Exodus 18:18 that Jethro saw burnout coming for Moses if he didn't change his approach to his job.

Many people suffer from one person's burnout. Jethro was not only concerned about Moses' well-being, he was also concerned about the people in Moses' care. Let's look again at what he says in Exodus 18:18: "You're going to wear yourself out—and if you do, what will happen to the people?" (TLB) Entire organizations, businesses, and nations suffer when leaders experience burnout.

When burnout occurs, its victims can no longer deal with people or handle daily problems (Num. 11:14-15). In the past Moses had successfully dealt with much greater problems and obstacles than the people's request for meat. But now he was emotionally overwhelmed. When people burn out, sometimes things that once would not have been major problems for them suddenly become impossibilities. They tend to make mountains out of molehills.

During burnout the person's relationship with God usually suffers (Num. 11:11). Notice what Moses tells God in Numbers 11:11: "Why pick on me, to give me the burden of a people like this?" (TLB) Moses was blaming God for his problems. During burnout we tend to lose touch with reality and try to find scapegoats for our problems.

God responds to the situation by promising that the people will have meat to eat every day for a month (Num. 11:18-20). In his burned out state Moses assumes he will have to do God's work for Him. Notice what Moses says when God promises to supply the meat.

There are 600,000 men alone [besides all the women and children], and yet You promise them meat for a whole month! If we butcher all our flocks and herds it won't be enough! We would have to catch every fish in the ocean to fulfill Your promise!" (Num. 11:21-22, TLB)

Moses had never responded like that before to God's promises. When God told Moses to hold his staff out over the sea so the waters would part and the people could cross on dry ground, Moses didn't say, "Hey, God, where am I supposed to put all the water left over when the dry ground appears?" He simply believed that God would solve all those problems and quietly obeyed (Ex. 14:16-21). But when Moses was burned out, he couldn't see any way for himself or God to carry out God's promise. In reality, he lost faith in God at that moment.

People experiencing burnout frequently give up on life (Num. 11:15). Moses tells God, "If You are going to treat me like this, please kill me right now; it will be a kindness! Let me out of this impossible situation!" (Num. 11:15, TLB) Moses wanted to escape, even if it meant death. This is a typical reaction of people experiencing burnout. They want to escape from the situations they are in because they feel they are no longer able to solve any of their problems or meet any of their goals.

THE TRAGEDY OF BURNOUT

When I was in junior college I played on the college basketball team. I worked hard to make the team and even harder to be one of the starting five players. I used to hate to sit on the bench while my teammates played the game. In fact, I would never voluntarily sit on the bench. Even though I might be exhausted, the only time I would sit on the bench was when the coach called me out of the game to rest. I had worked too hard to make the team to be content sitting by watching someone else play.

As we discussed earlier, people experiencing burnout have usually been high achievers. They have been part of the "starting five" in life. However, burned-out high achievers not only volunteer to sit on the bench—they quit the team and join the spectators in the stands. They become *watchers* instead of *doers*.

Neither they nor their "teammates" any longer reap the benefits of their talents and abilities. As a result, people with less capability fill in on the team, temporarily or permanently.

For example, Wayne Gardner, the former pastor of Hillside Community Church, is no longer pastoring a church. He is a real estate broker in Arizona. Not only are the people at Hillside Community Church missing Wayne's talents and ministry to them, but he is no longer using the abilities and gifts God gave him to pastor a church. As frequently happens with burnout, Wayne Gardner dropped out of his profession and so far has not returned.

Several years ago I lived in Alaska. While I was there, I met several people who at one time had been very successful business and professional people, but were now living lives of isolation in some small, rural villages in Alaska. Some of the communities didn't even have roads into them.

One man told me, "I'm here because I couldn't take the rat race any more. I was making $150,000 a year, but after twenty-five years with the same firm, I just couldn't take it any more." He went on to say, "I woke up in the middle of the night and decided to quit my job and come up here. The next morning I told my wife my decision, and she thought I was crazy." He laughed and said, "I'd have gone crazy if I had stayed in Chicago."

When I asked him what he was doing for a living, he said, "As little as possible. I do a little trapping in the winter and work for a sawmill in the summer."

IT DOESN'T HAVE TO BE THAT WAY

As I indicated earlier in the chapter, burnout can be a positive experience. It doesn't have to end the way it has for Wayne Gardner and the man from Chicago. It certainly isn't necessary to drop out of your profession or turn your back on life just because you burn out. I can speak from personal experience.

If you or someone you know is experiencing burnout, you need to realize that there is more than light at the end of the tunnel—the rest of your life is waiting to be lived. The lessons learned from burnout can make the future even more enjoyable than the past.

Even high achievers who have burned out and dropped out can come back and play the game of life and win! So take heart; if you are in burnout, there is hope for you.

BURNOUT WORKSHEET

This is not a test; it's a worksheet to help you determine if you have symptoms of burnout. For each statement choose a score ranging from 1–5, based on how closely you agree with the statement. A score of 1 means a very definite no, and a 5 means a very definite yes. Consider the past six months when giving your answers.

1. I seem to be working harder but accomplishing less. 1 2 3 4 5
2. I dread going to work each day. 1 2 3 4 5
3. I seem to have less physical energy than before. 1 2 3 4 5
4. Things irritate me that in the past didn't bother me............1 2 3 4 5
5. More and more I find myself trying to avoid people..........1 2 3 4 5
6. I seem to be getting more short-tempered......................1 2 3 4 5
7. I am having a harder time concentrating. 1 2 3 4 5
8. More and more I find myself not wanting to get out of bed in the morning. 1 2 3 4 5
9. I am starting to lose confidence in my abilities. 1 2 3 4 5
10. I am finding it harder and harder to concentrate on my work...........................1 2 3 4 5
11. It is getting harder for me to take risks................. ......1 2 3 4 5
12. I am becoming more dissatisfied with my accomplishments. 1 2 3 4 5

13. Lately I have started blaming God for my situation...........1 2 3 4 5
14. Some days I just want to run away from everything. 1 2 3 4 5
15. I care less and less if my work ever gets done or not.........1 2 3 4 5
16. It seems that everything is staying the same or getting worse. 1 2 3 4 5
17. It seems that everything I try to do takes more energy than I have. 1 2 3 4 5
18. I am finding it hard to do even simple and routine tasks...............................1 2 3 4 5
19. I wish people would just leave me alone......................1 2 3 4 5
20. I am frustrated with the changes I see in myself.............1 2 3 4 5

Scoring Your Burnout Worksheet

0–30 points = You are in no danger of burnout.
31–45 points = You are developing some of the symptoms of burnout.
46–60 points = You are probably starting to burn out.
61–75 points = You are definitely in the burnout process.
over 75 points = You are in the advanced stages of burnout.

This burnout worksheet is designed to give you some general guidelines for determining burnout. It is not a burnout test. After taking this inventory, if you feel you may have some of the symptoms of burnout, discuss it with a counselor.

Expanded versions of this burnout worksheet, designed to help you more clearly pinpoint the source of burnout, areas of your life it may be starting in, and the extent to which it has affected your life are available by writing Management Training Systems, P.O. Box 4779, Woodland Park, CO 80863.

TWO

TEN FACTORS THAT CAUSE BURNOUT

This country was founded on the Puritan work ethic. Historically, hard work has been considered almost synonymous with godliness. As a young nation the United States quickly gained the reputation of being the "land of opportunity." Hardworking, rugged individualists from all over the world flocked to this country by the tens of thousands to seek their fortunes and breathe the air of freedom.

Two hundred years ago 95 percent of the working people in America were self-employed. Even today many people still dream of starting and owning their own businesses. Throughout history the United States has been blessed with an abundance of self-motivated, goal-oriented high achievers.

This is not only the land of great opportunity, it is also the home of some of the most aggressive competitors in the world. That helps account for the fact that burnout is a much greater problem in this country than anywhere else in the world.

Burnout is the high price many people pay for high achievement. In this chapter we will look at the ten most common causes of burnout:
• Feeling driven instead of called
• Failing to pace ourselves
• Trying to do it all ourselves

- Excessive contact with people's problems
- Majoring on the minors
- Unrealistic expectations
- Developing too many routines
- An inappropriate view of God's priorities for our lives
- Poor physical condition
- Continuous rejection

FEELING DRIVEN INSTEAD OF CALLED

During the past several years I have provided management consulting and training services for a wide variety of Christian organizations. I have had the privilege of interviewing over 100 missionaries and twice that many pastors. I have also talked with countless Christian businesspeople about burnout. I have observed that Christians experiencing burnout frequently feel *driven* instead of *called*. They lose sight of the fact that God has placed them in the job or project and promised to provide everything they need to accomplish His will and purpose.

Instead, they feel compelled to do the job *for* God rather than let Him accomplish it *through* them. They rely on their own strength instead of God's. They wind up focusing on the activities instead of the ultimate purpose for the activities.

Mildred Bates was the choir director for a small church in Texas. She continually had trouble getting enough people together to keep the choir going. Frequently there weren't even enough people at choir practice to form a good quartet—let alone a choir. Because the church couldn't afford choir robes, Mildred organized a group of women in the congregation to make them. Mildred personally conducted bake sales to raise funds for sheet music for the choir. One week when the church organ needed repairing, she took money out of her own savings to get it fixed so it could be available to use with the choir the following Sunday.

When I met Mildred she was no longer choir director, and she was considering leaving the church. At the suggestion of her pastor she attended a seminar on burnout I was conducting.

During the coffee break she introduced herself and told me her story. "Last year's Easter cantata was the straw that broke the camel's back," she said. "I wanted to do *His Love Reaching* by Peterson, but I couldn't get enough people interested in the various parts. I finally got people from the community interested in singing in it, but the church board thought if we couldn't get enough interest from our own people we shouldn't have a cantata."

She shook her head and said, "I don't know what's the matter with our church board. We've had an Easter cantata for as long as I've been going to that church—and that is over ten years." Mildred explained that she had met with the board in an attempt to get them to change their minds about letting people outside the church sing in the cantata. "I turned in my resignation as choir director when they refused. And I'm looking for a new church!" she concluded angrily.

Mildred is a classic example of a person who was *driven* instead of *called*. She took things into her own hands and was determined to have a choir even when the people were not interested enough to sing in it. In reality it was Mildred's choir, not the church's or the Lord's.

Even though Mildred was adamant about having a choir, I never once heard her say anything about its spiritual value to the church. Nor did she discuss how it provided an opportunity for people to serve. She had totally lost sight of the purpose of the choir and was focusing only on the activity.

Once we lose sight of the purpose but continue to feel driven to perform the activity, we are prime candidates for burnout. When we feel driven to accomplish a task, we are actually violating God's Word, which says, "Work hard and cheerfully at all you do, just as though you were working for the Lord and not merely for your masters" (Col. 3:23, TLB).

This verse tells us we are to work cheerfully as well as hard. People who are driven to accomplish a task usually have an attitude that says, "I'll get this job done if it kills me!" And it just might. They are doing the job for the sake of getting the job done, not necessarily because they enjoy the job. Although they might have started out enjoying the work, as they became driven to do it, their satisfaction and enjoyment disappeared.

The verse also points out that we are to consider the work a "calling" from God: "just as though you were working for the Lord." People who are driven are doing the job for themselves—not for the Lord, even though they may not be aware of that.

Driven people are frustrated people, and people frustrated with their work will eventually burn out unless they resolve their frustrations.

FAILING TO PACE OURSELVES

High-achieving Christian leaders and businesspeople not only feel driven at times, but they also usually have problems pacing themselves. People who experience burnout have not learned to keep their lives in balance. Their friends usually refer to them as *workaholics* (and their families sometimes think about calling them names that are a lot worse!).

Before my own experience with burnout, my family and close friends kept telling me, "Myron, you need to slow down. You can't do it all in one day. You need to learn to relax a little." I brought work home every night and spent at least part of each weekend "trying to get caught up" in at least one of my businesses. However, I never got caught up. By the time one project was nearing completion, I was ready to start two more.

I went eight years without taking my family on a vacation. I traveled a lot with my work and just the thought of taking time off to take another trip wore me out. To ease my conscience, I would periodically take a long weekend off and take my family to visit relatives or friends. While they visited, I would try again to "get caught up" or use that time to think up a new project.

Many pastors and other Christian leaders have an even greater problem pacing themselves because of the pressures, importance, and "urgency" of their ministry. No one knew the importance and felt the urgency of the ministry the way Jesus Christ did. He came to seek and save the lost, and He had only three short years to accomplish all His work here on earth.

Notice how Luke describes the growth of Jesus' popularity and demands on His time: "Now the report of His power spread even faster and vast crowds came to hear Him preach and to be healed of their diseases" (Luke 5:15, TLB).

If Jesus had been like most high achievers, the length of His workday would have increased in direct proportion to the demands on His time. However, notice how Jesus handled His expanding ministry. "But He often withdrew to the wilderness for prayer" (v. 16, TLB).

As the demand on Jesus' time increased, He spent more time away for spiritual and personal renewal. He escaped from the pressures of the job and went away to the wilderness for time to relax and talk with God. He realized He couldn't continue to give of Himself without renewing Himself emotionally, physically, and spiritually.

If Jesus Christ needed to pace Himself and balance work with spiritual and physical renewal, think how much more we need to. Learning to pace yourself and keep a balance between your work, spiritual life, and leisure is the best insurance policy against burnout.

TRYING TO DO IT ALL OURSELVES

High achievers tend to have a great need for recognition. Often they feel they have to prove something to themselves or to someone else. The need to do it all is not always the result of not knowing how to delegate tasks to others, though that is certainly true in some cases. Frequently the high achiever wants to do all the work in order to gain recognition or approval.

For example, a good friend of mine, Bill, is currently going through burnout. He has been a very successful businessman and well-known Christian leader. I recently spent the day with him, and as we talked, he said, "All my life I've been trying to gain the approval of my dad. He always compared me with my other brothers—one has a lot more money than I do, and the other has a lot more education." Bill continued, "I guess I've tried to work harder and do more than my brothers in order to gain approval from my dad and my family. As a kid I would never let my older brothers help me do anything because I wanted Dad to see how well I could do things." Bill sighed and said, "The problem is that when I grew up, I never stopped needing to do it all myself."

There certainly isn't anything wrong with being an energetic, hard-working person. But it's asking for trouble to try to solve everyone's problems, provide all the answers, accomplish all the tasks, and do all the work. Most highly productive people aren't aware of their personal limitations—in fact, many of them don't think they have any. They continue to load themselves down with work, and because they are highly motivated and productive people, they get a lot accomplished. Their need for accomplishment drives them to do still more. Because high achievers tend to experience emotional highs from their achievements, they frequently have lots of energy.

But nothing can run forever without proper maintenance without breaking down. That is certainly true of people. People who always try to do it all themselves are headed for emotional and physical exhaustion—and that is what burnout is.

The high achiever should memorize Psalm 127:2: "It is senseless for you to work so hard from early morning until late at night, fearing you will starve to death; for God wants His loved ones to get their proper rest" (TLB). The person who tries to do it all usually winds up working from early morning until late at night. This verse points out that such a schedule is "senseless" because God wants us to get our proper rest. We all need emotional and physical rest. To avoid burnout, the high achiever must reject the temptation to try to do it all alone.

EXCESSIVE CONTACT WITH PEOPLE'S PROBLEMS

People who deal extensively with other people and their problems over an extended period of time are likely candidates for burnout. Almost all Christian leaders are prime targets for burnout because they deal continuously with people and their spiritual, emotional, financial, and relational problems.

Remember Wayne Gardner, the pastor of Hillside Community Church? Wayne found himself becoming spiritual shepherd and personal counselor to more and more people as time went by. Eventually he began to develop negative feelings toward people, and he grew to view people's requests for his time as "interruptions."

His constant involvement with people and their problems was directly responsible for Wayne's burning out and eventually leaving his pastorate.

The Apostle Paul was very much aware of the stress that results from constant contact with people. In his letter to the Galatians he wrote, "Let us not become weary in doing good, for at the proper time we will reap a harvest if we do not give up" (Gal. 6:9, NIV).

One of the reasons we "become weary in doing good" is that when we work with people, it often takes a long time to see positive results from our efforts. We are all slow to change. But we can change. That is why Paul said, "At the proper time we will reap a harvest if we do not give up."

As anyone knows who has tried, working with people requires a great deal of patience. Unfortunately, most high achievers are not noted for their patience. High-achieving Christian leaders frequently experience a great deal of stress—and sometimes burnout—when dealing with people, because they fail to see progress as quickly as they would like.

Numerous disappointments arise when dealing with people. People do not always make the changes we feel they are capable of making. Often, we conclude that their failure to change is because of our improper counsel or our inability to motivate them to change. Therefore, we feel that we have failed both them and ourselves.

MAJORING ON THE MINORS

When Wally Ferguson got out of trade school, he went to work in a shop repairing heating and air conditioning systems. A few years later he opened his own heating and air conditioning repair company. He worked hard and slowly built his business from a repair service company to a heating and air conditioning contracting business with a service department on the side.

When I first met Wally, he was one of the most enthusiastic and hard-working people I had ever seen. All he wanted to talk about was the heating and air conditioning business and how his company was expanding. Numerous building contractors in our city confirmed that Wally knew more about bidding heating and air conditioning jobs than anyone else in town. However, as Wally's business grew, he allowed himself to get bogged down in the day-to-day details of running the business.

Rather than hire a janitor or a janitorial service, Wally stayed after work each day and personally cleaned all the offices and the shop area. He told me, "Some people think I'm crazy for doing this instead of hiring someone to do it, but I figure as long as I have the energy I might as well do it and save the money." The same thing was true with the mechanical work on his trucks. Instead of sending his vehicles to a maintenance shop to have them worked on, Wally spent his weekends changing oil and washing and maintaining his trucks. He kept a typewriter in his office, and instead of letting his secretary type up all his bids, he did it himself. "I have to make sure these are done right," he told me. "One mistake could cost me the bid."

Wally was caught in the trap of majoring on the minors. He was bogged down in too many details that should have been done by someone else.

Recently Wally sold his business. He told me, "I just couldn't take all the hassle anymore. I couldn't find reliable help, and I didn't have enough time to properly prepare the bids. I started losing too many bids I shouldn't have lost."

He sighed and continued. "I have decided being in business for yourself just isn't worth the effort it takes. I'm fed up with people and the problems I had running the business. It is a whole lot easier working for the other fella and letting him deal with all the headaches."

Wally gives us a good example of what happens when a

person majors on the minors. He allowed himself to spend too much time and energy dealing with work and problems he should have delegated to others. His expertise was in figuring bids, not playing janitor. The little bit of money he saved doing his own janitorial and maintenance work cost him many times more in lost contracts because he didn't spend enough time on his bids. This led to emotional frustration, which finally caused him to throw up his hands and conclude that having his own business wasn't worth the hassle. Wally and many others like him could still be running their own businesses or involved in their careers if they had avoided majoring on the minors.

UNREALISTIC EXPECTATIONS

Most high achievers are not aware of their own limitations—in fact, they usually don't think they have any. As a result, they tend to set unrealistic goals and place excessive demands on themselves. They push themselves to the breaking point time and time again.

People who consistently set unrealistic or unattainable goals eventually get pretty upset with themselves. They don't understand why they haven't reached their goals. They start working even harder. The harder they work, the more frustrated they become, because they can never quite reach their goals.

Such people begin to see themselves as failures. Because high achievers cannot accept their failures, they eventually drive themselves to the point of total emotional, mental, and physical exhaustion as they try to achieve goals that were totally unrealistic to start with.

When the high achiever sets his or her goals too high, the failure to accomplish those goals creates frustration and leads to the development of a poor self-image. The failure to accomplish goals robs the high achiever of the positive feedback necessary for a high level of motivation. People need to experience success in order to develop and maintain a positive self-image.

The conference superintendent of one of our leading church denominations told me, "Many of our bright new pastors coming out of seminary burn out on their first pastorates because they have very unrealistic goals and expectations. They think they should be able to take a small, struggling church and transform it into the largest congregation in the city during their first couple of years there. Many of them actually wind up dropping out of the ministry because they fail to meet the demands and goals they place on themselves. As a result they get frustrated and decide they just aren't cut out for the job."

"It is not good to have zeal without knowledge" according to Proverbs 19:2 (NIV). High achievers usually have plenty of zeal, drive, and energy. But they frequently lack the wisdom to set personal goals. Unrealistic expectations are almost sure to ensure eventual burnout.

DEVELOPING TOO MANY ROUTINES

During a workshop on burnout Sandra Green said, "When I started my job, I was so excited. It was the kind of job I had always wanted. But eventually I got so depressed and frustrated with it that I had to quit." She went on to say, "Every Monday I worked on billings. On Tuesdays I worked on sales commissions. On Wednesdays I did the payroll. It was the same old thing week after week. I dealt with the same people and the same problems all the time."

She laughed and said, "In fact, my whole life became one boring routine. Monday evenings I did the laundry. Wednesday evenings I went to church and Friday evenings I had sex with my husband whether I was in the mood or not."

Routines sap the challenge and excitement out of our lives. They destroy our creativity and turn innovative people into robots. People who allow too many routines to develop in their lives have taken the first step toward burnout. They are *letting* things happen instead of *making* things happen. They are on the road to apathy, and apathy is a close cousin to burnout.

On the other hand, routine can be good if it leads to the formation of positive habits that free up our conscious minds to work on more creative endeavors. Some vocations are subject to a great deal of routine. We need to learn to make the routine work for us by using the mental time that routines provide to think about more creative activities. Otherwise, we may find burnout waiting for us around the corner.

AN INAPPROPRIATE VIEW OF GOD'S PRIORITIES FOR OUR LIVES

Many Christians, and especially Christian leaders, have an inappropriate view of God's priorities for their lives. God's work becomes *their* work. They aren't actually working for God; they are working for themselves.

They also allow their work for God to create a lack of balance in their lives. They justify neglecting their families by the importance of the ministry. Their whole lives revolve around *their* ministries. They eat, sleep, breathe, and talk ministry. All of their friends are involved in the ministry. If they go on a weekend outing, it is with their peers in the ministry. If they play a game of tennis or golf, it is with people from the ministry. If they have guests for an evening, it is to discuss the ministry.

I have had the opportunity to work with many such people. Unfortunately, they usually do not believe they have a problem. In fact, they are often very self-righteous because of their "commitment and dedication" to the ministry. However, such people are on a collision course with burnout. Their lives are out of balance. It is only a matter of time till they become mentally, emotionally, physically—yes, and even spiritually—exhausted.

POOR PHYSICAL CONDITION

It was Vince Lombardi, the former coach of the Green Bay Packers, who said, "Fatigue makes cowards of us all." Poor physical condition is one of the major causes of burnout.

It is very easy for high achievers to push beyond their physical limits. Because high achievers have lots of drive and energy, they must keep their bodies physically fit in order to keep up with their mental and emotional drives. In order to try to cram in extra meetings I have driven all night on several occasions, gone without proper rest, skipped meals all day, and so on. This type of schedule is common for high achievers.

I have observed in my own life that when I neglect my physical needs I am much more vulnerable emotionally and mentally. Good physical health is one of the best ways to protect against burnout. We must be physically healthy in order to maintain our emotional and mental well-being.

CONTINUOUS REJECTION

Lloyd Dobson used to sell pots and pans door to door. He told me, "I made a decent living, I had a good product, and I loved meeting new people. But I finally had to quit door-to-door sales because I couldn't take all the nos it took to get the yeses I needed."

Henry Hudson manages a large department store for one of the major chains. Not long ago he told me, "Our greatest employee turnover problem is in our customer complaint department. If I leave a person in that job too long they'll quit because they can't take the constant complaints and hassles people give them day after day. I've learned to rotate people in that area. The first day or two they can handle any customer problem, but after a few days they start to get irritated at the least sign of dissatisfaction displayed by the customer. At that point I know I'd better move them back out on the floor or I'll lose them."

People dealing with continual rejections are prime candidates for burnout. Too many rejections cause us to develop negative attitudes toward people, our jobs, and ourselves.

The problem comes when we take rejection personally. We need to realize that people are rejecting our products or services, not ourselves. If we understand that, we won't be beaten by rejections, rather we will be challenged to meet them head on.

THREE

FORCES CONTRIBUTING TO BURNOUT

In addition to the ten factors mentioned in the previous chapter, there are several other forces that contribute to the development of burnout, including our society, our jobs, our personalities, and our temperaments. Let's look first at our society's influence.

OUR SOCIETY'S CONTRIBUTION TO BURNOUT

Competition in our society. We in the United States live in one of the most competitive societies in the world. That helps explain why burnout syndrome is a greater problem here than in other countries.

High achievers are by nature very competitive. One never reaches high levels of achievement by being willing to settle for average performance. In fact, high achievers usually feel like failures even when they finish in second place.

I remember my first real taste of competition. At the ripe old age of six I entered a footrace at the county fair with other kids my age from all over the county. I wasn't a very big kid, but I could outrun all the other first graders in my class. In fact, I could even outrun all of the second graders and a lot of the third graders.

I had never lost a race with anyone my own age. But that

39

day at the county fair I came in second. First I felt surprised that someone my age could run faster than I could, because it had never happened before. Then I remember feeling very sick inside when I realized I had been beaten—I hadn't won the race.

After the race was over, one of the judges lifted the kid who had beat me onto his shoulders for everyone in the crowd to see, and they cheered and applauded. As the judge put the winner back on the ground, he handed him a gold trophy. Even though I came in second, only a couple of steps behind the winner, all I received was a pat on the head and a small red ribbon with gold letters spelling the words "second place."

Lots of kids were gathered around the winner looking at his bright, gold trophy and patting him on the back. Someone from the newspaper was there to take a picture of the winner with his trophy. As I walked off the track, only two or three of my friends were there to greet me. Bruce, my best friend, said, "That's OK, Myron. He was a lot bigger than you."

But my friend's efforts to comfort me didn't make me feel any better. I wadded the ribbon up, stuck it in my pocket, went over among the parked cars where no one could see me, and cried. That day I learned several things: society loves a winner; there is always someone with a little more natural talent; and I hate to lose. That race at the county fair was my first official step into the competitive society we live in. I quickly learned that competition is a way of life.

Within a few years I was competing to make the grade-school basketball team, then the high school team; even later I competed for a position on a college basketball team. I competed for grades in school, for part-time jobs while working my way through college, and eventually for a full-time job after graduating from college. As a businessman I found myself competing with others for business and qualified employees.

Everywhere we turn in our society we face competition. For the high achiever, competition is one of the great motivating factors for success. It can also become one of the forces pushing us toward burnout.

High achievers love the challenge of competition. The

greater the competition, the harder they work to overcome it. As a result, over an extended period of time the highly competitive forces at work in our society can cause high achievers to push themselves to their physical and emotional limits—and into the clutches of burnout.

Madison Avenue's false image of success. Another force working in our society is the hype created by advertisers concerning success. Media Avenue would lead us to believe that success and happiness can be measured by the number of things we can afford to purchase and the size of the price tags attached to them. People frequently fall into the trap of accumulating large quantities of material possessions only to discover that they don't really provide true happiness, nor do they represent real success.

Jack Ackens was such a man. I met Jack at a workshop on burnout I was conducting, and the next day he invited me to lunch. "I have spent my whole life building a financial empire," he said. "I suppose only my accountants really know what I'm worth."

Jack spent the next half hour telling me how his mother had raised a family of five boys and four girls during the Depression by taking in laundry, cleaning houses, and working nights in a bakery. "I grew up determined to have all the things the rich folks had in the houses my mother cleaned," Jack said. "And with a lot of hard work and a little luck I have made a lot of money during my lifetime."

Jack began describing his real estate holdings, mining businesses, and foreign investments. He owned several of the most expensive cars in the world along with two summer homes— one in Hawaii and the other in Vail, Colorado.

Before lunch was over, however, I learned that Jack Ackens was a very tired, frustrated man who had literally burned himself out making money and acquiring material possessions only to discover at the age of sixty-two that they really didn't provide the happiness he had expected. As we talked, I became acquainted with a very lonely, hurting, physically and emotionally exhausted man inside that expensive suit and silk shirt. He had been married and divorced three times and was currently living alone. His children refused to visit him, even at Christmas, and he had contemplated suicide several times during the past year.

Unfortunately, there are numerous Jack Ackenses across this country. Maybe they haven't accumulated quite as much wealth as Jack has, but they are working at it full time. And, like Jack, they are likely candidates for burnout. They too will discover that the Madison Avenue approach to success and happiness will fail to produce the desired results.

Pressure on homemakers to work outside the home. Women working outside the home represent one of the largest groups of people experiencing burnout in our country today. Historically it was thought that burnout syndrome was a problem associated primarily with men in executive positions. However, in recent years large numbers of homemakers, including mothers—especially those working outside the home—have been experiencing burnout.

These women often feel pressure to do all of the housekeeping tasks, no matter how busy they get. When a couple has children, the woman's work load is greatly increased, but the husband may or may not lighten that load by assuming some of the homemaking responsibilities.

As the family grows, so do the financial obligations. The family needs a bigger home, two or more cars, money for schooling—the list goes on and on. The wife frequently works full time outside the home during the day to help meet mounting costs, yet she may still be expected to be a full-time mother, cook, housekeeper, and lover when she comes home at night.

Therefore, it is easy to see why working mothers are currently among the most susceptible to burnout. They, as much as anyone else in our society today, are subject to all of the factors that cause burnout.

The rapid pace of our society. Never before in our history has a society moved at such a rapid pace as ours. For thousands of years of recorded history the civilized societies of the world relied on the horse as their "rapid" transportation. In the past few generations all of that has changed.

In the past hundred years our society has moved from horseback to space travel. Information that a few short years ago took months to gather can now be collected and analyzed in a matter of seconds by sophisticated, high-speed computers. Satellite communication now makes it possible for us to sit in our own homes and watch events on TV as they are happening halfway around the world.

Most of us would agree that modern technology has allowed us a more enjoyable lifestyle, but it has also created additional problems. Our modern, fast-paced, rapidly changing society has become a breeding ground for the stresses that help produce burnout.

Trying to keep up with the Joneses. Trying to keep up with people around us is another force in our society that contributes to burnout. By nature high achievers do not like to be outdone. They feel compelled to do things better than their peers. If the neighbor puts in nice landscaping, she wants hers to look nicer. If a fellow employee buys a new car, he wants a better one.

The end result can be enormous financial strain. This pressure can drive a person to work even harder in an effort to pay for the cost of keeping up with—and ahead of—the Joneses. Such pressure also helps contribute to the physical and emotional strain that eventually leads to burnout.

HOW OUR JOBS CONTRIBUTE TO BURNOUT

The average working person spends about 40 hours a week on a job. That represents approximately one fourth of the 168 total hours in a week. Most high achievers, on the other hand, spend 50–60 hours a week on the job. That can come to more than one third of their time each week.

In addition, the average jobholder can usually forget about the job on evenings, weekends, and other times away from work. The high achiever usually takes work home in the evenings and frequently spends part of the weekend working on and thinking about work-related projects and activities. The high achiever generally expends much more mental and emotional energy on the job than do others in the work force.

Climbing the organization's career ladder. No matter how low on an organization's career ladder high achievers start, they set their sights on one of the top positions in the organization as a goal for the not-too-distant future. Because of their strong abilities, they usually begin moving up the career ladder more quickly than other less aggressive employees.

However, the closer to the top of an organization one gets, the fewer the positions available and the greater the competition for them. Plus, at the upper levels of an organization's career ladder, everyone is a high-achieving, aggressive person, so the competition is even greater.

There are only a few top slots in any organization, so not all high achievers will reach their career ladder goals. Failing to reach those goals can certainly set the wheels in motion for burnout.

Feeling inadequate because of job-related, technological information gaps. As we mentioned earlier, our society is in the midst of a technological explosion. This creates information tidal waves and the need for continual updating and education on the part of employees.

It is not uncommon for students fresh out of college to be more familiar with the latest technological advancements than seasoned employees who have worked in the field for years. Rapid technological advancement coupled with the flood of information can create feelings of inadequacy in all employees— especially high achievers. High achievers working in fields where there is rapid technological change find themselves always playing catch-up, and burnout often results.

Poor managers and supervisors. Managers and supervisors of high achievers frequently play a major role in high achievers' burnouts. For example, high achievers can make less motivated supervisors feel threatened. As a result, supervisors may try to control the power of such high achievers by limiting their decision-making authority or the types of projects they are allowed to work on.

This can be very de-motivating to high achievers. They feel

their talents and abilities are not being used effectively, which can create tension that can eventually lead to personality conflicts. The already high job-related stress is compounded by tension with managers and supervisors.

Not enough job flexibility. High achievers are frequently very creative people. They usually need new challenges on a regular basis. If their jobs limit flexibility or have too many routines, high achievers can become bored and frustrated. As we have already seen in a previous chapter, this too creates stresses that can eventually lead to burnout.

PERSONALITY AND TEMPERAMENT TRAITS

Personality and temperament traits play a major role in the development of burnout. High-achieving burnout-prone people usually share many personality and temperament traits. Let's look briefly at how each of these traits contributes to burnout.

They are strong willed and determined. People who are strong willed and determined hate to give up and admit defeat. They frequently push themselves to their physical and emotional limits in an effort to make things happen. As a result they often pay a high physical and emotional price for success.

They are decisive. High achievers are decisive. They are not afraid to make decisions, even when they lack all the facts. As a result, they do not always make the best decisions, but they are willing to make up for weak decisions with hard work. This means they frequently have to work harder for their achievements than necessary because their impatient natures have led them to act prematurely.

They tend to be self-sufficient. High achievers usually would rather do things themselves than take the time to show someone else how to do them. As a result they frequently get bogged down in details that could and should be done by someone else. They also tend to waste time figuring things out for themselves instead of asking for help. But again they make up for the loss of time by working that much harder to get the job done. And they feel good about themselves when they are able to do it without asking for help from others.

They are very self-confident. One of the reasons they don't ask for help is because they know they can get the job done one way or the other. They are very sure of their own abilities and tend to trust their own judgment over the judgment of others. They can point to long histories of success, including how they succeeded where others had failed. It becomes more and more easy for them to rely on themselves instead of others.

They are frequently perfectionistic. High achievers usually maintain very high standards of performance for themselves and others. They hate sloppy workmanship and strive to do and to be the best at whatever they attempt. Therefore, they frequently place more demands on themselves than others would place on them. They expect more and better performance from themselves than others would expect. They put undue pressure on themselves to perform "above and beyond the call of duty."

They are usually well organized. High achievers have plans and are working with all the energy they can muster. They make things happen instead of letting them happen. They know not only where they are headed, but how to get there. Their lives are orderly and purposeful, and they hate chaos and "wheel spinning." They have a purpose in everything, and they never experiment "just to see what will happen."

They frequently resist regulations. High achievers tend to feel boxed in and under pressure when required to live according to too many regulations and rules. They want and need the liberty to be flexible and improvise in order to get their jobs done. As a result, they frequently become frustrated when required to work within the confines of organizational rules, regulations, and standard operating procedures. They feel a great need to be able to do things their own way.

They are positive, optimistic, and enthusiastic. They have great faith in themselves and their abilities. They tend to look on the bright side, even in the face of adversity. This sometimes causes them to keep working on a project long after it should have been abandoned.

They are very goal oriented. High achievers don't get where they are by accident. They have purposes and causes in life and goals to operate by. However, because their goals are not always realistic (even though they may accomplish them), they frequently push continually in an effort to meet excessively high goals. Their high energy levels and determination usually make it possible to achieve their goals, even though they pay a high physical and emotional price in the process.

They are usually independent and sometimes loners. As we have already seen, they would rather do their jobs themselves than ask for help. They tend to work alone and independent of others. They frequently have difficulty becoming team players.

They are willing to take risks and thrive on challenges. High achievers are generally not afraid of the unknown. They tend to work on the cutting edge of society where there is always the chance of both great rewards and serious losses. Such an environment helps provide the extra motivation sometimes needed in order to turn something average into something great.

They are highly competitive. High achievers not only want to win, they *must* win. They are usually willing to pay any price necessary to succeed. Burnout frequently becomes the high price paid for such high levels of winning and achieving.

They thrive on achievement and the recognition it brings. Many high achievers have an excessive need to achieve because they feel, deep down, insecure. They use their achievements to build their confidence and a positive self-image. This can lead to a very unhealthy need for achievement and cause them to push themselves beyond their limits.

They need to be in control. High achievers have a strong need to be in control, and they don't give up control easily. They want to be in charge of their own destinies. They have a hard time turning loose and letting others share in the responsibilities and rewards.

They hate failure in themselves and others. High achievers can't stand the thought of failure. They go to great lengths to ensure success. They are willing to pay almost any price to avoid failure—and the price most often paid is the physical and emotional fatigue of burnout.

Looking at the personality and temperament profile of high achievers, it is easy to see that they are frequently their own worst enemies. Their personalities and temperament traits have embedded within them the root causes that lead to burnout.

FOUR

SYMPTOMS OF BURNOUT

According to society's standards Paul Jenkins is a highly successful businessman. When I first met Paul, he was forty-one years old and owned two summer homes in the mountains, a large sailboat, three sports cars, two ranches, seven sporting goods stores, and several large commercial office buildings. At his invitation I met Paul and his wife for dinner one evening to discuss the expansion and management needs of his retail sporting goods business.

Halfway through the meal Paul said, "I don't know why I keep talking about expansion. What I really want to do is sell out and move to the ranch and just forget it all." For the next two hours Paul poured out his frustrations with his business, his employees, himself, and life in general.

All his life Paul had been a high achiever. He was named all-American two years in a row during his college football days and was offered an opportunity to play professional football. Paul was a perfectionist and was determined to be the very best at whatever he did. He decided to go into business instead of playing professional football and opened seven very successful sporting goods stores in six years.

During our conversation Jan, Paul's wife, said, "Paul has the capacity of two or three people. Before he completes one project he has started four or five more. And he always makes them work."

Paul looked at his wife and gave a half-disgusted grunt. "You're talking about the 'old' me. Now all I want to do is get out from under all this pressure and go off and hibernate."

As he played with his napkin he continued. "It's all I can do to drag myself out of bed in the morning. And when I do get up I'm usually more exhausted than when I went to bed."

He shook his head in frustration and said, "I just don't know what's the matter with me. I work harder and accomplish less than anyone I know. Just last week I told Jan that if I could find a buyer I'd be willing to sell my business for half of what it's really worth—I just want out."

The longer Paul talked the more irritation showed in his voice and facial expressions. Finally he said, "Look! Let's just stop talking about the business and try to enjoy our meal. I've made a decision. I'm not going to expand—I'm going to sell! And so let's just forget about the business."

As I sat listening to Paul and Jan that evening I realized that Paul had all the symptoms of burnout. I was sitting across the table from a man who had run out of gas emotionally, mentally, and physically. I didn't know he was a Christian at the time, but I later learned that his burnout had caused him to dry up spiritually as well.

One doesn't need to be a trained psychologist or psychiatrist to detect that a person is experiencing burnout. Just as there are identifiable factors that cause burnout, there are also recognizable symptoms that alert us to its presence. In this chapter we will take a close look at those symptoms.

TYPES OF BURNOUT SYMPTOMS

There are two types of burnout symptoms—*external* and *internal.* External symptoms of burnout include
• Activity increases but productivity initially stays the same.
• Irritability
• Physical fatigue

- Unwillingness to risk

Internal symptoms of burnout include

- Loss of courage
- Loss of personal identity and self-worth
- Loss of objectivity
- Emotional exhaustion
- Negative mental attitude

We will look at the external symptoms of burnout first. These are visible symptoms that can be observed in the person going through burnout. They are usually the first clues we have that people are experiencing burnout.

Internal symptoms of burnout are invisible at first and are therefore harder to detect. However, they are the ones that provide the most accuracy in diagnosing burnout. They tend to precede the external symptoms.

EXTERNAL SYMPTOMS

Activity increases but productivity initially stays the same. One of the first external symptoms of burnout is an increase in activity without a corresponding increase in productivity. As burnout begins to develop, expected results no longer occur, and the high achiever increases his or her activity to compensate for the loss of productivity.

Jim Ander, one of my former business partners, has helped numerous salespeople overcome burnout. He once told me, "I can watch the production reports of our salespeople and tell when a person is starting to go into burnout." He went on to explain that the salesperson starting into burnout begins to experience a decrease in sales. He said, "To compensate for their drop in sales they ask for more appointments, but their levels of sales don't increase accordingly."

I saw the same pattern develop in my own experience with burnout. As emotional exhaustion set in, my level of productivity dropped. To compensate for that, I started taking work home in the evenings, going to the office on Saturdays, and staying late at work in order to catch up on the things I couldn't seem to get done during the day.

My increase of activity only added to my already building frustration with the job, because even though I was working harder, I didn't seem to be getting any more accomplished. In fact, I seemed to be getting further and further behind.

That is exactly what happens to the person experiencing burnout. More activity to make up for the drop in productivity only adds to the frustration that led to the drop in productivity in the first place. The result is like throwing gasoline on a fire—you end up with a bigger fire. And the more a person starting to burn out increases activity, the faster the burnout occurs.

People in burnout become irritable. Another external symptom of burnout is that the victim becomes irritated with things that were never bothersome in the past. During my dinner meeting with Paul and Jan Jenkins, Jan said, "Until recently Paul could handle any kind of pressure. But lately it seems that everything bothers him."

"That's true," Paul chimed in. "In the past I could roll with the punches, but now I'm ready to punch anyone who makes a mistake. I just don't know what's the matter with me."

As Paul and Jan talked, I thought of both Moses and Jeremiah In chapter 1 we saw how Moses went through a period of burnout. The same thing happened to Jeremiah (see Jer. 20:7-18). Both Moses and Jeremiah became irritated with both God and the people they were working with. In Numbers 11:11 Moses asked God, "Why have You brought this trouble on Your servant? What have I done to displease You that You put the burden of all these people on me?" (NIV) And in Jeremiah 20:7 Jeremiah told God, "You deceived me. . . . You overpowered me. . . . I am ridiculed all day long; everyone mocks me" (NIV).

People experiencing burnout become irritated at themselves for lack of personal accomplishments, at others for hindering their accomplishments, and at their jobs because they are at the center of their frustrations. If the person is a Christian, he or she becomes irritated at God for allowing all of the problems to occur.

Physical fatigue. Continually being tired is another external symptom of burnout. Sandra Webber was a bored homemaker. She went to real estate school and within five years had her broker's license and owned the most successful real estate company in her city. Her husband once told me, "She's a bundle of energy and ideas. She isn't happy unless she's solving someone's problems in order to make a real estate deal work."

However, Sandra recently called me in tears. "I have finally accomplished all of my goals for the business. Things are going great at the office and business has never been better," she said through her tears. "But lately all I want to do is stay in bed. Here it is two o'clock in the afternoon and I've only been out of bed an hour today—and that was to fix John's lunch."

Sandra thought she was experiencing some type of physical sickness, but she was actually going through burnout. Remember in chapter 1 that we defined burnout as "the type of stress and emotional fatigue, frustration, and exhaustion that occurs when a series of (or combination of) events in a relationship, mission, way of life, or job fail to produce an expected result." Sandra had developed a very successful business, but it hadn't met her needs or made her happy. She became frustrated with the business and began to experience the stress and emotional fatigue characteristic of burnout.

It was Sandra's emotional fatigue that produced the physical exhaustion and tiredness. People in burnout have exhausted all of their emotional and physical energy.

Burned-out people no longer take risks. High achievers are by nature risk takers. High achievers are also very competitive and thrive on challenges. But when burnout occurs, the previously high-achieving risk taker becomes fearful of risks, loses that competitive spirit, and runs from problems.

People in burnout want to escape instead of facing the challenges of the job. They are consumed with wanting to "run away to the mountains," or "run away to the farm." They want to get away from people, the pressures of the job, and their friends and hide from the rest of the world. A line in a popular song summarizes the attitude of the person in burnout when it says, "Stop the world and let me off. I'm tired of going 'round and 'round."

The reason people in burnout will no longer take risks is that they have lost faith in themselves and their ability to achieve. They see themselves as failures and develop a negative outlook on life in general.

As I indicated earlier, Paul Jenkins opened seven successful sporting goods stores in six years. He was a risk taker as well as a good businessman. However, during my dinner with Paul and Jan, Paul said, "I'm afraid to try to open another store in this part of the state. And I'm not sure I could effectively manage one if it was too far away geographically."

When I suggested relocating one of his assistant store managers and promoting him to store manager of the new store, Paul shrugged his shoulders and said, "I just don't think it would work. It would be too risky the way the economy is right now."

Even though Jan tried to point out to Paul that he had opened stores and made them go when the economy was a lot more unstable than it was then, Paul would not budge. He couldn't bring himself to take the risk.

INTERNAL SYMPTOMS

People in burnout lose their courage. One of the reasons people in burnout are unwilling to take risks is that they lose their courage. High achievers are normally strong people. They have a great deal of confidence in themselves and their abilities. But the emotional, mental, and physical exhaustion that produces burnout turns strong, courageous people into cowards.

In fact, most people going through burnout reach a point at which they want to give up on life itself. For example, in Numbers 11:14-15 Moses told God, "I can't carry this nation by myself! The load is far too heavy! If You are going to treat me like this, please kill me right now; it will be a kindness! Let me out of this impossible situation!" (TLB)

Notice what Jeremiah told God in Jeremiah 20:14-18.

"Cursed be the day that I was born! Cursed be the man who brought my father the news that a son was born . . . because he did not kill me at my birth! Oh, that I had died within my mother's womb, that it had been my grave! Why was I ever born? For my life has been but trouble and sorrow and shame" (TLB).

David also responded with despair in the midst of his burnout. "My heart is in anguish within me. Stark fear overpowers me. Trembling and horror overwhelm me. Oh, for wings like a dove, to fly away and rest! . . . I would flee to some refuge from all this storm" (Ps. 55:4-8, TLB)

This is the same David that killed a lion and bear with his hands and went against the giant, Goliath, with a slingshot and five smooth stones. This is the man of which the people in Israel said, "Saul has slain his thousands, and David his tens of thousands" (1 Sam. 18:7, NIV). Yet in the midst of burnout David lost all his courage and, like Moses and Jeremiah, just wanted to escape and not deal with life. This is one of the key internal symptoms of burnout.

The loss of personal identity and self-worth. The loss of personal identity and self-worth is another important internal symptom of burnout. People going through burnout lose their senses of identity and self-worth because they suddenly realize they can no longer match their previous levels of achievement and performance.

The boundless energy they once had is gone. Where once nothing could stop them from succeeding, they now feel that it is impossible for them to reach even the smallest goal. Once they had a positive outlook on life and their activities, but now they are convinced that nothing will work out right.

Their purpose or cause in life is gone. They have stopped setting goals and objectives, because they are convinced they can't achieve them anyway. Their concern for people has turned into contempt. And, if they are Christians, their love for God has turned into apathy.

As these feelings, attitudes, and changes occur in these once-high achievers, they realize that they no longer know or trust themselves. The achievements, contributions, and high levels of performance from which they developed their personal identities and self-worth in the past are all gone.

Their friends, acquaintances, and business associates have started to question their reliability as well. Where they were once the catalysts, motivators, and innovators of activities, they now feel as if they are no longer needed or wanted.

The once highly motivated, goal-oriented, self-starting high achievers in burnout become listless and lifeless, meandering aimlessly from one day to the next. They no longer know who they are or where they are headed in life, and they don't much care, because they no longer feel capable of making any meaningful contributions.

People in burnout lose their objectivity. People in burnout lose their objectivity and make decisions based on their emotions rather than on facts. This is the third internal symptom of burnout.

High achievers become successful because they learn to make the right decisions at the right time. However, burnout victims lose the ability to operate on facts and sound principles. Instead they operate and make decisions on the basis of feelings. This is one of the reasons their levels of performance begin to slip.

Moses is a classic example of a person in burnout losing the ability to remain objective. In Numbers 11:18-20 God promised the Children of Israel they would have meat to eat every day for a month.

Notice Moses' response to God's promise. "There are 600,000 men alone [besides all the women and children], and yet You promise them meat for a whole month! If we butcher all our flocks and herds it won't be enough! We would have to catch every fish in the ocean to fulfill Your promise!" (Num. 11:11-22, TLB)

Moses was upset with the people and their continuous complaining. In his burned-out state he couldn't be objective or realistic when God promised to feed the people meat. Moses' emotions got in the way of God's promise, and he was trying to figure out how he, Moses, was going to provide the resources to fulfill God's promise. His conclusion was that it was impossible.

God had to jolt Moses back into reality by pointing out that Moses' ability to supply the meat was not a prerequisite for God's promise being fulfilled (Num. 11:23). In his highly emotional state of mind, Moses had lost sight of that fact.

Because people going through burnout lose their objectivity, their decisions change as often as their emotions and feelings. It is hard for people in burnout to make and stick with decisions. It is not uncommon for people in burnout to make a decision, but before it is carried out, reverse that decision and go in the opposite direction with their actions. They appear to others to be unstable—and they are.

People in burnout are emotionally exhausted. Emotional exhaustion is another internal symptom of burnout. Notice again David's statement in Psalm 55:6-8. "Oh, for wings like a dove, to fly away and rest! I would fly to the far off deserts and stay there. I would flee to some refuge from all this storm" (TLB). David was emotionally and physically exhausted. He couldn't deal with the pressures of his duties anymore. He wanted to go off to a faraway desert *and stay there.*

David gives us a good example of the results of emotional exhaustion. He wanted to run away to some isolated place and stay there in order to escape from people and the day-to-day pressures of his responsibilities. I have observed in my own experience with burnout—as well as in counseling with many other people in burnout—that emotional exhaustion tends to produce the desire to escape from the present situation to some quiet, isolated spot far away.

It is the emotional exhaustion that produces the inability to cope with the day-to-day pressures, problems, and situations of the job or business. Emotionally exhausted burnout victims simply do not have any more strength to handle even the smallest problems. They conclude that the only solution is to run away from the situation.

People in burnout have negative mental attitudes. By nature high achievers usually have a very positive outlook on life and a practical, realistic view of situations. They tend to be very flexible people who are capable of rapid recovery from failures. As they begin experiencing burnout, however, their attitudes become more and more negative until finally their outlook on life is predominately negative. They are no longer able to bounce back from failures, setbacks, rejections, and problems.

In burnout, every problem, rejection, or failure—no matter how slight—reinforces the negative attitude and serves to "prove" that the burnout victims are no longer capable of achievement or making meaningful contributions. It is this negative mental attitude that keeps high achievers down once they have fallen, and the longer they are controlled by negative mental attitudes, the harder it is for them to pull out of burnout.

FIVE

MAJOR CONSEQUENCES OF BURNOUT

Elijah, that great prophet of God and man of faith of the Old Testament, gave a timeless summary of the end result of burnout in just three words when he said, "I've had enough" (1 Kings 19:4, TLB). Every person in burnout eventually reaches that conclusion and, like Elijah, says, "I've had enough! I quit!" I call it "the Elijah decision," and everyone who goes through burnout ultimately makes that decision.

THE "ELIJAH" DECISION

The Elijah decision is the decision to give up on everything in life that has been important. It means giving up on your purpose in life, all the goals you've had, and all the things you've worked so hard for. When people in burnout make the Elijah decision, they are giving up their faith and trust in their friends and peers. Finally, they are giving up on themselves, God, and life in general.

I clearly remember my own Elijah decision when I was in the midst of burnout. Everything that had been important to me in life was gone. The marriage I had worked so hard at for those twenty-three years was gone. The businesses I had started and sweat great drops of blood for now belonged to someone else. I felt my closest friends had turned their backs on me in my time of greatest need. I was numb from emotional exhaustion.

All of that caused me to walk into my little apartment one day, toss my coat over the back of a chair, turn and lock the door, take the phone off the hook, close the drapes, slump down in an overstuffed chair, close my eyes, and say, "God I've had it! I quit! Why don't You just let me die right here in this chair!"

I had made my Elijah decision. Like Moses, Jeremiah, and Elijah, I had given up. I wanted to die.

The Elijah decision represents the depths of despair in burnout. It is the culmination of the following major consequences of burnout:
- Loss of purpose in life
- Having one's self-image destroyed
- Feeling and alone in the world
- Being filled with resentment and bitterness
- Feeling that all is hopeless

There are certainly other consequences of burnout that could be listed. However, these represent the major factors that contribute to a person's arriving at the decision to give up on life and eventually wish he or she was dead.

LOSS OF PURPOSE IN LIFE

High achievers are persons of purpose. They not only know where they are headed and how to get there, but they also know *why* they are doing what they are doing. Purpose tells us *why* we do the things we do. It is our cause in life.

People with a purpose in life make things happen. Those without a purpose let things happen. People with a purpose in life are willing to face any adversity. Those without a purpose aren't willing to try anything for fear of adversity.

Purpose in life is to the high achiever what rocket fuel is to a spacecraft—it provides the energy and power for success in the mission. People aren't high achievers because of natural talent (though they may be very talented). Their achievement is due to a purpose in life that motivates them to pay the price—no matter how high—for success.

The greatest motivating force in the world is purpose in life. A purpose to live for or a cause to die for enables people to reach levels of achievement and perform heroics that others consider impossible.

I recently went to see my family doctor for a physical checkup. As he checked my blood pressure, tapped my knee to see if there was any life left in me, and looked in my ears for my brain (or whatever they look for in there), we discussed the important role purpose plays in a person's life.

As we talked, he said, "The reason so many people die within a year or two after they retire is that they no longer have a reason to get out of bed in the morning. They don't have a purpose to live for."

When he said that, I immediately thought of my own experience with burnout and the experience of others in burnout I had counseled. One of the reasons people in burnout make the Elijah decision and wish they could die is that they too have lost their reasons to get out of bed in the morning. I remember that on numerous occasions I found myself still in bed at three or four in the afternoon during my bout with burnout—and I didn't even feel guilty. However, before my burnout experience I almost considered it a sin if I wasn't up to watch the sunrise. Even on Saturdays I would try to get my family up at the crack of dawn to tackle some weekend project (even if that project was nothing more than a trip to the local donut shop).

A very successful businessman in our community, a close friend of mine, is currently suffering from a severe case of burnout. Not having heard from him in several days, I called his office one afternoon to see how he was getting along. When his secretary told me he hadn't been in all day, I immediately called his home.

As I talked to his wife on the phone, she said, "Myron, I don't know what's the matter with Bill. He's been in bed all week. I've tried to get him to go to the doctor, but he refuses."

As I talked to Bill on the phone I heard a man who had lost his purpose in life. He said, "You know, Myron, I can't believe what's happened to me. I don't have any enthusiasm for my work anymore. In fact, I hate going to the office. It seems I just run from one problem to the next down there."

There was a long pause on the phone before Bill continued. "Quite frankly, I'm to the point where I don't care if the work gets done or not. If some of my employees can't get the job done, it might not get done at all."

The longer Bill talked the more he raised his voice. "I'm tired, Myron." He sounded as though he was pleading for help. "I just want to quit. I just want out. Do you know what I mean?"

I did know what Bill meant. I had been there. I knew the feeling—the loss of meaning and purpose in everything in life.

Many times during seminars on burnout I have been asked, "How do people who have been high achievers suddenly lose their purpose in life?"

First of all, let me say that it doesn't happen suddenly. But in order to answer the question, let's look again at the definition of burnout as stated at the beginning of the book. Burnout is the type of stress and emotional fatigue, frustration, and exhaustion that occurs when a series of (or combination of) events in a relationship, mission, way of life, or job fail to produce an expected result.

Let's look very closely at the definition. The key phrase is the last one—*"fail to produce an expected result."* That doesn't necessarily mean the person failed. In the eyes of others the person may be very successful. Goals may have been achieved. Profits may be up. People in the relationships may be getting along fine, and so on. However—and this is very important to note—the results did not produce *what the burnout victim expected.*

For example, my friend, Bill, the businessman who had lost his purpose in life, was staying home in bed instead of going to the office. Bill once told me he had wanted to go into business for himself because he wanted to be his own boss and control his own time. Bill was a very successful businessman. He had a lot of money, had a reputation for being honest, invested his money wisely, and maintained a very affluent lifestyle. However, all his success in business failed to produce the result he expected—control of his own time.

In fact, just the opposite occurred. The bigger Bill's business grew, the more demands there were on his time. Instead of having more time for himself, Bill discovered that he had less and less. What he had wanted to happen and had expected to happen as a result of building a successful business never occurred.

For that reason, Bill began experiencing stress, emotional fatigue, frustration, and finally exhaustion—physically, mentally, and emotionally—because the harder he worked, the less time he had for himself. And time for himself was the reason he was working hard in his business in the first place. The end result? Bill simply wore himself out and gave up. He concluded that he could never achieve his real goal, so he quit altogether.

HAVING ONE'S SELF-IMAGE DESTROYED

The second major consequence of burnout is the loss of a positive self-image. Self-image is one of the most important elements of our emotional and psychological makeup. It influences our personalities, what we do, and how we live. Self-image plays a big part in determining the kind of cars we drive, clothes we wear, and houses we live in. In fact, it helps determine our actions and achievements in all areas, including our careers, who our friends and acquaintances are, whom we marry, our financial success, and even our relationship with God.

When we say, "I could never see myself doing that," we are actually admitting that the image we have of ourselves prevents us from doing that. As long as we can't see ourselves wearing that, doing that, driving that, living there, working there, achieving that, and so on, we won't do those things.

Self-image is derived from how we feel about ourselves, how we perceive others feel about us, and how we think God feels about us. Self-image is based largely on approval and acceptance. If we feel God and other people approve of us and accept us as we are, then it is easier for us to approve of and accept ourselves. The result is a positive, healthy self-image. High achievers tend to have more positive self-images than low achievers. This fact is magnified greatly in a highly competitive, achievement-oriented society.

But the perception of failure is always associated with burnout. In fact, it is at the very core of the burnout process. As mentioned earlier, the person going through burnout may not have failed at all, but he always perceives himself as having failed.

In the last chapter we pointed out that people going through burnout develop a very negative attitude because they are no longer able to bounce back from what they consider failures, setbacks, rejections, and problems. As the burnout victim concludes he is failing, his self-image begins to deteriorate. The more frequent and greater the failures, the more his self-image is undermined, so that by the time the person in burnout makes his Elijah decision, his self-image is totally shattered.

In the midst of burnout, I sat on the bed one day thinking, *I've got to find a job, but what can I do?* As I scanned the want-ad section of the paper, I first looked at the various executive and management positions listed. But I thought to myself, *I could never do that!* even though I had started three successful businesses of my own and worked as a consultant for a number of large organizations in the area of management and organizational development.

Eventually I found myself looking at janitorial jobs. I thought, *Maybe I could do that, but I'm not sure I could handle the pressure of having to be at a job every day.* Finally I spotted an ad for part-time drivers to deliver pizzas. Even though I thought I might be able to handle that job because it was only part-time, I didn't call because I was afraid I would be turned down and not get the job.

I closed the paper and sat on the bed and began to cry. For the first time during my struggle with burnout I realized how low my self-image had fallen and what little self-confidence I had left. In the past I had thrived on challenges and believed I could solve almost any problem and overcome any obstacle to achieve a goal. But now I didn't even have enough faith in myself to think I could qualify as a part-time pizza deliveryman. I was a classic example of a burned-out person with a devastated self-image.

The burned-out person believes that he is no longer capable of making any positive contributions. It is this totally negative self-image that causes the person in burnout to ultimately develop a death wish. When Elijah told God, "I've had enough. Take away my life. I've got to die sometime, and it might as well be now" (1 Kings 19:4, TLB), he was actually admitting just how low his sense of self-worth really was. He had decided that it was impossible for him to do anything for God or the nation of Israel. He believed he was worthless and might as well die now since death was inevitable for all people anyway. Elijah's feelings are typical of the feelings of people in burnout who are unable to cope with shattered self-images.

FEELING ALONE IN THE WORLD

People experiencing burnout begin to feel totally isolated and alone in the world. The simple fact is that they usually are alone since they tend to isolate themselves from others. People in burnout withdraw from other people, even those closest to them, because they are unable to cope with what they feel are serious failures and their growing negative self-images.

Even those with extroverted personalities want to hide from people during burnout. I have always been very people oriented. However, when I was experiencing burnout, I frequently wouldn't even answer the phone when it rang. I would agree to have someone over to my apartment just for a friendly chat and maybe some dessert and then turn out the lights, lock the door, and go to bed before my guest arrived simply because I couldn't face him or her.

The isolation and feeling alone go hand in hand, creating a self-fulfilling prophecy. People in burnout feel they don't have any friends left—but they refuse to let anyone be a friend.

Russell Perkins, a very dear friend of mine, is currently going through a severe case of burnout. Recently I called Russell every day for two weeks in a row trying to get him to go to lunch with me. Each day he had a flimsy excuse as to why he couldn't make it that day. Russell's wife told me, "Russell sits around all the time complaining about how none of his friends ever come around any more, but he won't talk to them when they do. Lately he won't even talk much to me or the kids. It seems he's just crawling further and further back into his shell."

Their desire to escape the reality of what's happening to them is part of the reason people in burnout withdraw from those around them. They have not only lost their purpose in life and suffered serious blows to their self-images, but as we saw in the last chapter, they have also lost their sense of courage. They feel they simply don't have the strength left to face any of life's situations. All they want to do is run and hide.

Every person going through burnout can identify with David's statement when he said, "Oh, that I had the wings of a dove! I would fly away and be at rest—I would flee far away and stay in the desert; I would hurry to my place of shelter, far from the tempest and storm" (Ps. 55:6-8, NIV).

A well-known pastor friend of mine recently told me of his experience with burnout. "I just wanted to run as far away from people as I could," he said. "I couldn't stand the thought of standing up in front of my congregation, looking them in the face, and preaching another sermon."

He went on to explain that he felt so guilty about his attitude that he finally resigned, moved his family into a smaller house, and moved himself into a tent on some property he owned in the mountains of western Colorado. "I spent four years up in the mountains building a log cabin and trying to sort things out in my head," he told me. "On several occasions I thought about committing suicide, but I never did because I was afraid that if I tried but didn't die I'd really be in a mess up there in those mountains alone. I learned one thing through that experience. Running away and hiding from people is not the way to get out of burnout!"

BEING FILLED WITH RESENTMENT AND BITTERNESS

As we have already seen, the person experiencing burnout usually has been a very goal-oriented, high-achieving, and productive individual. He has been a positive thinker who thrived on a challenge. But he seems to become a totally different person in burnout. Instead of being goal oriented, he now has no purpose in life. Where he once thrived on a challenge, he now runs from life, wanting to hide from the world. And even though he was once a positive thinker, he is now negative, resentful, and bitter.

Notice the resentful, bitter tone of Moses' statement to God during his experience with burnout. "Why pick on me, to give me the burden of a people like this? Are they *my* children? Am I their father? Is that why You have given me the job of nursing them along like babies until we get to the land You promised their ancestors?" (Num. 11:11-12, TLB)

That same attitude is also noticeable in Jeremiah when he told God, "O Lord, You deceived me when You promised me Your help. I have to give them Your messages because You are stronger than I am, but now I am the laughingstock of the city, mocked by all" (Jer. 20:7, TLB).

The resentment and bitterness experienced by people in burnout is focused in three directions: at themselves, at other people, and at God. They are angry and bitter toward themselves because they see themselves as total failures. They resent other people because they feel that it was the people around them that caused them to fail. And they are bitter and resentful toward God because they feel that somehow He let it all happen.

This resentful, bitter spirit is one of the most damaging of all the consequences of burnout. It fosters an attitude of hatred and rebellion. It causes the person in burnout to falsely accuse others. And it usually blinds him to his own mistakes, weaknesses, and shortcomings, which led to burnout in the first place.

As we will see in a later chapter, the burned-out person's greatest spiritual battles usually revolve around his feelings of resentment and bitterness. These feelings and attitudes make it very difficult for the person going through burnout to be honest with God, himself, and others. Yet such honesty is absolutely essential in order to recover from burnout.

During my own struggle with burnout some of my greatest battles were fought trying to overcome deep-seated feelings of bitterness. I still carry some of the scars of those battles to this day. As I fought these battles, I sought out the help of many professional counselors. I talked to friends and poured my heart out to various members of my family. But I soon discovered that only God could help me win the battle against the strong feelings that had a stranglehold on me and my emotions. Later in the book we will devote an entire chapter to discussing how God works in us and for us to deliver us from the clutches of burnout.

FEELING ALL IS HOPELESS

People in burnout are convinced that they will never succeed at anything. *So why try?* they wonder. They become complacent with life because they feel that all is hopeless. Where once they felt nothing was impossible, now they feel nothing is possible.

While I was going through burnout, I discovered that every time someone tried to encourage me with a positive solution, I always found some reason why it wouldn't work. In talking with others in burnout, I have seen that same pattern in them.

One of the reasons people in burnout feel that everything is hopeless is that deep down inside they want it to be hopeless. By that I mean that they don't want to change. Change means risking failures, and they can't handle any more failures. They would rather do nothing than run the risk of another failure.

Not long ago a woman approached me at the conclusion of a workshop on burnout and asked to talk to me in private. After I had put my training materials away, we went to a coffee shop and she told me her story. She had been a nurse for almost thirty years and had held supervisory positions in some of the nation's largest hospitals. "About five years ago I realized I was starting to burn out, but I couldn't seem to do anything about it," she said. "Finally I quit my job, but by then I was having trouble in my marriage and I just sort of became a hermit. Now my husband is threatening to leave me. My kids say I'm so negative they don't want to be around me anymore. I just don't know what to do."

As we talked I offered several suggestions, but each time she would shake her head and give me an excuse for why it wouldn't work. Finally I asked, "Do you really want it to work, or are you just wanting someone to feel sorry for you?"

She looked at me, and tears started streaming down her face. She said, "I'm afraid. Everything seems so hopeless. I can't work. I can't please my husband. I can't get along with my friends. And now my own kids don't even want to be around me."

As we had a second cup of coffee, I learned that she had been offered several jobs but had turned them down. Her husband had been trying to get her to go with him to a marriage counselor. But she had refused to attend counseling sessions with her husband.

She said, "I didn't take the jobs because I was afraid I wouldn't be able to handle them and I'd get fired. And I don't want to go to a counselor because I don't want them probing into my private life."

In reality, she really didn't want to run the risk of doing things that could help her come out of her burnout syndrome. She had concluded that things were hopeless, and she was doing everything she could to prove she was right. Unfortunately, until she is willing to take that first step forward in her life, it will remain hopeless.

But no case of burnout is *really* hopeless! There are tested and proven steps to recovery, and I can speak from experience that the lessons learned in burnout can make you an even stronger and more effective person.

SIX

TIPS FOR RECOVERING FROM BURNOUT

When I think of the process involved in recovering from burnout, I am reminded of two friends of mine, Roger and Peggy Glenville. Several months ago Roger and Peggy returned home from shopping one Saturday afternoon to the horrifying scene of fire fighters battling a blaze that was rapidly destroying their home. Flames and large billowing puffs of black smoke seemed to be engulfing one entire end of the house and the attached garage.

After what seemed an eternity to Roger and Peggy, the fire was put out, and later they and the fire marshal began assessing the damage. "Our home is ruined!" Peggy cried, as they walked across the newly installed carpet in the family room that was now flooded with a black mixture of water and ashes.

The fire marshal tried to console them by explaining that the damage wasn't actually as severe as it appeared on the surface and that a good contractor could have the home repaired as good as new in far less time than they might think.

Roger called me that night and told me about the fire, and after church the next day he and I drove over to look at the damage again. I had to admit that the house looked in very bad shape to me, and I questioned whether it was salvageable. The entire end of the two-story house, along with half of the garage, appeared to have been destroyed. One entire wall of the garage was completely gone, the roof was partly burned, and the end of the house was charred black.

The inside of the house looked even worse. The walls, ceiling, and all of the contents were totally covered with a heavy film of black grease from the smoke. The carpet and furniture were still soaking wet from all the water sprayed into the house by the fire fighters.

I looked at Roger and asked, "What did your insurance agent say?"

He shook his head and replied, "He said they wouldn't have a total estimate of all the damages for a couple of days, but he assured me they would have a construction company fix it just like new."

I didn't say anything to Roger, but I didn't see how that was possible. However, during the next few weeks I got the surprise of my life.

Every few days I drove by Roger and Peggy's house to see what progress the construction company was making in its attempts to fix up the house. First they tore out all the area damaged by the fire and hauled it away, including the carpets and damaged furniture inside. Then they built entirely new walls and a new roof section. They completely repainted the interior and exterior of the whole house and totally redecorated the interior, including new carpets and drapes in every room. The insurance company paid for replacing all the damaged furniture. As the fire marshal had predicted, within a few weeks Roger and Peggy's old, burned-out house looked like a brand new home inside and out.

There are many parallels between the fire that burned Roger and Peggy's home and human burnout. As I watched with amazement the workers rebuilding the Glenvilles' home, I was reminded of my own recent experience with burnout and the rebuilding of my personal life.

Just as I was convinced that it would be impossible to repair Roger and Peggy's burned-out house, I had also believed I would never recover from burnout. As I watched the burned-out shell of the Glenvilles' home being reconstructed board by board into a beautiful new home, I remembered how my own burned-out emotions had been rebuilt little by little and piece by piece until I was—as the fire marshal had promised the Glenvilles—"as good as new." And if you are experiencing burnout, you also can become as good as new.

YOU WILL NEED HELP IN OVERCOMING BURNOUT

As we saw in the case of Moses when his father-in-law Jethro came to visit him, burnout victims would rather do things themselves than ask for help. But no matter how talented, motivated, or capable a person is, he can't always do everything alone. This certainly applies to recovering from burnout.

Jim Ander, a marketing and sales expert and former business partner of mine, has dealt with many burnout cases while holding various sales manager positions. In fact, Jim was the first to recognize my problem with burnout, and he played a major role in my recovery.

One day Jim invited me to lunch and very tactfully began to describe the symptoms of burnout to me. "I see many of these symptoms in you, Myron," he told me. I didn't want to admit it at first, but eventually I had to agree that Jim was right.

"I'll start working on my problems," I told him.

He just shook his head and said, "No, Myron. It won't do any good for you to try to solve this thing by yourself." Jim went on to explain to me that he had dealt with burnout in countless salespeople and that he had never seen even the most strong-willed victims solve their burnout problems on their own.

Being rather hard-headed myself, I laughed and said, "Well, maybe I'll be the first." But I quickly learned that Jim was absolutely right. I tried to set new goals for myself, but I couldn't generate enough motivation and energy to start working on them. I would get up in the morning and tell myself how great a day I was going to have, but by noon my strong feelings of hopelessness had usually convinced me that it was going to turn out to be the worst day of my life. The more I tried to solve my problems on my own, the more frustrated I became. I found myself trying to analyze my every thought and action. I became harder and harder on myself until finally I had to go back to Jim and admit to him that he was right. I hated to admit it, but I did need help to lick this thing—I couldn't do it alone.

THE TYPE OF HELP YOU WILL NEED

Many people think that they must attend expensive counseling sessions with a psychiatrist or psychologist in order to recover from burnout, but that is not necessarily true. The person in burnout will, however, need someone to counsel them who thoroughly understands burnout and the process involved in recovering from it. If a qualified nonprofessional is not available, professional counseling will probably be necessary. Whoever counsels the person in burnout must have a great deal of patience but at the same time be firm and hold the person in burnout accountable.

ACCOUNTABILITY

The first prerequisite to recovering from burnout is to be willing to submit yourself to someone else and become accountable to that person as your counselor. For the strong-willed former high achiever this can be a serious problem; it is easy for pride to get in the way.

It is very difficult for people who were once independent, productive high achievers to admit that they can't solve their own problems. Chances are they once prided themselves in being able to handle any problem, large or small. But now they are in a situation in which they can no longer handle themselves.

I clearly remember how difficult it was for me to go back to Jim Ander and admit I couldn't solve my own problems. It was even harder to be willing to ask him for help and then make myself accountable to him. But I can't emphasize enough how important this is in the process of burnout recovery.

No matter how disciplined a person was before becoming burned out, he will find that during burnout he has become very undisciplined. Therefore, the person in burnout must have someone to help set goals and then hold him accountable for their completion. Remember: *the burnout recovery will only be successful insofar as the person in burnout is willing to become accountable to a counselor.*

The person doing the counseling must keep in mind that the person in burnout may have a hard time being held accountable. For example, while Jim Ander was working with me in overcoming burnout, I became a master at developing excuses for why I couldn't or didn't do what he required. I also on many occasions conveniently forgot appointments with him because I didn't have my assignments completed. Jim was always understanding, but he never let me off the hook. For instance, he quickly learned that the surest way to meet me for a luncheon appointment to discuss my progress was to pick me up at my apartment and physically take me to lunch.

Recovery from burnout requires a two-way commitment. Not only is it important for the person in burnout to make a commitment to the counselor, but it is essential that the counselor make an equal commitment to the person going through burnout. In fact, in the early stages of burnout recovery, the counselor's commitment is frequently much stronger than that of the person who is experiencing the burnout.

PITFALLS TO AVOID

Don't expect too much too soon. This applies to everyone involved including the person in burnout, his family and close friends, and the counselor. The person going through burnout was a high achiever in the past, the type of person who jumped into a project and generally completed it ahead of schedule, but that person has changed. He is physically, emotionally, mentally, and spiritually exhausted. He has lost faith in his ability to achieve anything.

I learned from my own experience, and I have observed it

countless times in others, that it is very easy to expect too much too soon when dealing with burnout. The day Jim agreed to work with me to overcome my burnout I thought to myself, *In a few days I'll have this thing whipped and have the old me back.*

I quickly learned that I didn't want the old me back. It was the old me that had led to this mess and gotten me into burnout in the first place. I had to learn how to have balance in my life. I had to learn when to quit, when to say no to challenging projects that I shouldn't be involved in, how to relax and unwind, where my personal limits were, and finally what my real priorities in life should be.

People experiencing burnout must realize that there is no quick fix or shortcut to overcoming burnout. It takes takes time, patience, and commitment on everyone's part.

Don't expect things to be what they were before. The goal in overcoming burnout is to correct old, bad habits and learn some new, good ones. Burnout recovery requires making changes in the way you think, the things you do, how you do them, and even why you do them.

After burnout recovery has been completed, you will live your life differently. That doesn't mean you will no longer be the goal-oriented, productive, positive, high achiever you were before. You will have the potential to accomplish even greater things than before without fear of burning yourself out, but the way you accomplish them will be dramatically altered. The way you live your life and spend your time will be drastically different.

During burnout recovery you will learn the difference between "working hard" and "working smart." You will discover how to pace yourself instead of always driving yourself. And you will discover that knowing how to relax and play hard is just as important as knowing how to work hard.

HELPING THE FAMILY RECOVER FROM BURNOUT

The person going through burnout isn't the only one who suffers and needs help. Alcoholics Anonymous, that fine organization that for years has been helping alcoholics rebuild their lives, learned a long time ago that it wasn't enough to just work with the alcoholic—they also had to help the family of the alcoholic recover from the destructive effects alcohol had had on the entire home. The same is true with burnout. The person suffering from burnout is not the only victim of burnout. The entire family suffers as well. Burnout causes a great deal of frustration, pain, and grief to members of affected families. In many instances burnout leads ultimately to divorce.

The family members have been living with the person going through burnout. They have watched the high achiever turn into an unproductive emotional basket case right before their eyes. They were the ones trying to remain calm and collected in the midst of the storm of confusion and chaos created by the person in burnout. The family of the one going through burnout has its own hurts, scars, and emotional needs that must be healed and restored.

I first met Bud and Kay Hillery at a burnout workshop I conducted in my hometown. After the workshop was over, the Hillerys asked me if I was available to go to a local restaurant for coffee and dessert. As we finished our pie and ice cream and started our second cups of coffee, Kay turned to Bud and said, "Are you going to ask him, or should I?"

Bud ran his fingers over the design of the tablecloth and finally looked up at me and said, "I think I'm going through the burnout you described tonight. Do you think you could help me out of it?"

For the next two hours I sat and listened first to Bud and then to Kay as they told their story—one that has been duplicated so many times across this country. Bud owned one of the largest construction companies in the city. By hard work, determination, and what we call in the business world "guts," he had worked his way up from a common laborer to the owner of a successful business. Bud was the classic example of the fulfillment of the American dream. The Hillerys had been very active in the church for years. Kay taught a Sunday School class and sang in the choir, and Bud was a member of the church board.

"On the surface we look like we're doing great," Kay said, "but inside we're both starting to come apart."

I looked at Bud and he confirmed Kay's analysis. "That's about right, Myron," he said. "I'm so burned out I feel like I've been fried to a crisp." He tried to muster a laugh, but somehow no one thought it was very funny.

I agreed to start working with Bud to help him overcome his burnout and soon learned that Bud's burnout had created serious problems at home also. Bud told me, and Kay agreed, that he had never been a violent person prior to experiencing burnout. However, a few months ago he had gone into a rage during an argument with Kay and hit her.

"I felt terrible when it happened," Bud said. "I told her I was sorry and asked her and God to forgive me, but things just haven't been the same since." I later learned that Bud had also threatened to leave Kay on several occasions and had actually spent the night in a motel after one of their arguments. Kay was planning to take their two children and go to her mother's home and file for divorce. At that point I met with both Bud and Kay and asked them if they were willing to see a marriage counselor or meet with their pastor for help with their marriage. They finally agreed, and for the next six months I worked with Bud in his burnout recovery while their pastor helped them put their marriage back together.

Bud and Kay provide a good example of how a person's burnout ultimately affects the entire family. Not long ago I bumped into Bud and Kay in a shopping mall. It was like a family reunion. Kay threw her arms around me and said, "You know, if we hadn't asked you out for dessert after your workshop on burnout that night, I'm sure Bud and I would not be together today." They are still together, and with God's help and the aid of a couple of counselors, they have rebuilt a strong marriage and Bud has won his bout with burnout. I wish all of the cases ended that way, but unfortunately many of them don't. Counselors who attempt to help people overcome burnout need to be sensitive to the needs of the whole family, not just those of the burnout victim.

FAMILY MEMBERS' ROLES

Those closest to the person in burnout, such as family members and close friends, play a very important role in the burnout victim's recovery. Their attitudes and actions during this time are very important. I would like to share some do's and don'ts for family members to consider in helping a loved one recover from burnout.

•Always communicate that you still believe in the person.

•Love the person even when he or she is not lovable.

•Show interest in the person's assignments and progress.

•Let him know it's OK to blow it.

•Don't put pressure on the person to succeed.

•Don't preach.

•Don't try to replace the counselor as the authority.

Always communicate that you still believe in the person. The counselor working with the person in burnout has the task of helping rebuild his or her self-confidence. But the family and friends of the burnout victim also need to let him know they have not lost their faith in him. They should consistently communicate that they still believe in his abilities and that he will once more become a productive, fulfilled person.

Without regular reinforcement from my family I'm not sure I could have recovered from burnout. They called, wrote letters, had me over for dinner, and made up a thousand excuses to see me in order to say, "Myron, hang in there. You're going to make it. We still believe in you." Their faith in me helped me to begin believing in myself once more.

Love the person even when he or she is not lovable. First Thessalonians 5:15 says, "Make sure that nobody pays back wrong for wrong" (NIV). People in burnout can be very difficult to live with or be around. They frequently take out their frustrations on those closest to them. It is easy to want to strike back and get even when we are wronged, but if we truly want to help those in burnout successfully recover, we must love them even when they are not lovable.

Bud Hillery told me, "I think I could have made better

progress recovering from burnout if Kay hadn't been threatening to leave me all the time." He went on to explain that the turmoil at home compounded the frustration and emotional exhaustion he was already feeling and made it even more difficult to concentrate on anything positive.

"I saw our deteriorating marriage as just another proof that I could no longer do anything right," Bud said.

Kay agreed that her lack of love and support during the early stages of Bud's recovery made things much more difficult for him. She said, "I guess I was hurting so bad I wanted him to have to suffer along with me."

They both agreed that as Kay began showing more love toward Bud there was a marked improvement in the rate of his recovery.

Show interest in the person's assignments and progress. The more interest you show in the individual's assignments and progress the more you are communicating your support. People in burnout need to know they are being supported in their efforts to overcome burnout. The larger the "cheering section," the greater the potential for recovery.

Football game announcers on television frequently talk about "the home crowd advantage" during the game. They point out that a highly supportive and vocal home crowd is often as valuable as having a twelfth player on the football field would be. The same applies to the person trying to win the struggle with burnout. Those on the sidelines can have a major role in the burnout victim's success by showing their support.

Let him know it's OK to blow it. As we have frequently mentioned, the person in burnout feels like a failure. Family members and friends can help soften emotional blows and discouragements due to lack of progress or mistakes during burnout recovery by letting the individual know it's OK to fall short of the expected goal.

We must keep in mind that one of the reasons people experience burnout is that they have had a tendency to drive themselves too hard toward unrealistic goals. During burnout these people had a tendency to expect too much too soon.

Therefore, they may frequently bite off more than they can chew unless properly guided by a counselor.

When this occurs they will be very tempted to give up; failure will be seen as one more proof that recovery is hopeless. Since one of the consequences of burnout is feeling that everything is hopeless, it is very important to communicate to the person attempting to recover from burnout that it is OK when he blows it. Things are not hopeless, and recovery from burnout will be a reality if the person doesn't give up.

Don't pressure the person to succeed. The more pressure burnout victims feel to succeed, the more frustrated and upset they will be if they fail. As family members and friends encourage them, they should be very careful not to overdo their enthusiasm to the point that the victim feels undue pressure from them.

Looking back on my own experience with burnout, I can assure you that the person attempting to recover from burnout is already under pressure from within to succeed. Family and friends should relax and encourage the burnout victim to work toward recovery at a reasonable pace.

Don't preach. During my struggle with burnout, well-meaning friends, acquaintances, and even strangers shoved countless stacks of books under my nose, offered all kinds of advice, suggested causes of my problems, and lectured me by the hour on what I should and should not be doing. In counseling with others who have gone through burnout, I have discovered that they experience much the same thing.

The person trying to overcome burnout certainly doesn't need sermons and lectures from anyone—and especially not from family members and close friends. That does not mean you should never offer advice or give suggestions, but always avoid preaching and lecturing. That will only add to the burnout victim's frustrations.

Don't try to replace the counselor as the authority. It is very important for family members to trust the counselor to do the counseling job. Assuming the person counseling the burnout victim understands burnout and the recovery process, the person in burnout only needs one counselor for burnout. (He may need help in other areas, such as with his marriage, but he should have only one counselor for burnout recovery.) When well-meaning family members and friends also try to start counseling the burnout victim, usually all they accomplish is confusion, and they run the risk of undermining the very important trust relationship between the counselor and the burnout victim, which is so important for a successful recovery.

SEVEN

COMPLETING THE RECOVERY PROCESS

We live in the age of the "miracle drug." Medical science has made giant leaps forward in finding cures for illnesses and diseases that only a few short years ago were considered incurable. Almost any organ in the body can be successfully transplanted, including the heart.

We have also been programmed to expect instant results. We enjoy, and take for granted, everything from fast food restaurants to quick-copy printing shops. We used to be happy when the photo shop told us we could get our pictures developed in two or three days, but now we expect to have our prints in less than an hour. Over the past few decades we have become a society that demands instant cures and fast results.

With all our medical and technological advancements, however, we have made very little progress in reducing the time it takes to recover from emotional trauma. There are no quick fixes or shortcuts when dealing with the aches and pains caused by emotional frustrations and fatigue.

It takes time to recover from burnout. We may go to work in the morning feeling fine and come home that night with a bad case of the flu, but that isn't the way we develop burnout. It occurs over an extended period of time (sometimes months or even years) as stresses and frustrations brought on by our failure

83

to see expected results slowly sap our strength and bring on physical, emotional, and mental exhaustion. Just as it takes time to develop burnout, it also takes time to recover from it.

No two persons are alike, and no two persons' burnout experiences are identical. However, just as there are common causes and symptoms of burnout, there are also standard procedures, principles, and methods for recovering from burnout. In this chapter we will look at a proven step-by-step process for successfully recovering from burnout syndrome.

SEPARATE YOURSELF FROM THE SOURCE OF THE PROBLEM

The first step in burnout recovery is to remove yourself from the source of the burnout. If you place your hand on a burning stove your hand will continue to burn until you remove it. Even though you still feel the pain for a while after you remove it from the stove, it slowly stops hurting. The same is true of burnout. You can never recover from burnout as long as you remain in the situations that caused the burnout. It is imperative that you remove yourself from the "heat" before recovery can begin. This is always the starting point in the recovery process.

This may seem like a simple and obvious first step, but for most people it is a very difficult one. There are many issues to confront and questions to ask at this point.
•How far must I be removed?
•For how long must I be removed?
•Who fills my place while I'm gone?
•Will I ever be involved in the same situations again?
•What will I do while I'm gone?
•How can I afford to be removed?

As you can see, the list can go on and on, and the answers are not always readily available. This is one of the reasons many people never escape from burnout. They become trapped in situations and circumstances and don't know whom to turn to for help.

Most of the steps presented in this chapter are not optional.

They are essential for successful recovery. This first step is certainly no exception.

Even our subconscious minds know how important it is to get away from the source of the burnout. As they attempt to communicate this need to us, our conscious minds tell us to "run" or "escape to some isolated spot" away from the cause of the problem. All people in burnout develop the feeling that they want to just run away and hide from the world. Part of the reason for this is that they *do* need to get away from the source of the problem.

This can be accomplished in a number of ways. An employer may assign the employee in burnout different responsibilities or transfer him or her to a different department or even different geographic location. Sometimes it is possible for an employee to change shifts, so that he is working with different people in a new and different atmosphere. Since every person's burnout experience is different, I can't tell you exactly what is best suited for you. But I can assure you that burnout recovery will not be possible unless you separate yourself from the source of the problem! How this separation occurs is something that must be worked out between the counselor and burnout victim as they consider the circumstances involved.

HAVE A TIME OF REST AND RELAXATION

It is impossible to deal with burnout victims' emotional exhaustion as long as they are physically exhausted. Physical exhaustion must be dealt with first. This principle is clear from the way God helped Elijah during his time of burnout. Elijah told God, "I've had enough. . . . Take away my life. I've got to die sometime, and it might as well be now" (1 Kings 19:4, TLB). Elijah was definitely experiencing a severe case of burnout. In the verses that follow notice how God deals with Elijah's burned-out condition:

> Then he lay down and slept beneath the broom bush. But as he was sleeping, an angel touched him and told him to

get up and eat! He looked around and saw some bread baking on hot stones, and a jar of water! So he ate and drank and lay down again. Then the angel of the Lord came again and touched him and said, "Get up and eat some more, for there is a long journey ahead of you." So he got up and ate and drank, and the food gave him enough strength to travel forty days and forty nights to Mount Horeb (1 Kings 19:5-8, TLB).

Like other people experiencing burnout, Elijah was physically exhausted. After telling God that he was giving up on life and that he wanted to die, he lay down and went to sleep. Notice that God didn't come along and say, "Hey, Elijah! What's the big idea goofing off on the job? I've got big plans for you, so get up and get going!" No. God sent an angel to feed Elijah. God knew he was physically exhausted and needed to rest and be physically restored before he would be of any good to anyone. We don't know exactly how long Elijah was at the broom bush resting, but it must have been a considerable length of time, because God had to send the angel more than once to feed him. Like Elijah, people experiencing burnout must have a time of rest and relaxation to overcome their burned-out condition.

This is also a very hard step for people in burnout. They are not accustomed to getting away for times of rest and relaxation. In fact, they probably do not know what the word *relax* means! Their lives have been full of action and activity—and now I'm telling them to relax! In most cases, they won't even know where to start.

At this point the counselor plays a very important role. He must not only get the burnout victim to agree to make arrangements to get away for a time of rest, but he must make sure the person in burnout knows what to do to relax. Notice that I said, "get away." If at all possible, he should get out of town on a vacation to a quiet place away from the phone and the hustle and bustle of lots of people.

When Jim Ander gave me the assignment of taking some

time off and getting away to rest, I said, "Jim, I can't afford to do that." He looked me squarely in the eye and said, "Myron, the way I see it, you can't afford not to. Do you want to recover from burnout, or do you want to spend the rest of your life wasting away and miserable?"

I tried to argue with Jim, but he wouldn't back down. I had to get away and relax. When I agreed to a two-day trip, he made me extend it to two weeks.

But Jim didn't just send me away on a two-week trip. He was much smarter than that. He gave me a list of do's and don'ts to be religiously followed.

•Pick a place that is quiet but has facilities for recreational activities, such as swimming, golf, tennis, horseback riding, fishing, and hiking.

•Take along a Bible, as well as some light reading material.

•Make a commitment not to use the time to try to solve your problems or figure out what to do. Remember, you are going there to rest and relax—nothing more!

•Don't take any work with you from your job.

•Don't call the office or other people from work while you are gone.

•Avoid reading newspapers and listening to or watching the news on TV. You are there to enjoy a time of relaxation, not fill your mind and thoughts with the problems of the world.

•Do something different each day. Don't just play golf or just go fishing.

•Try things you have never done before. For example, if you don't know how to play tennis—learn.

•When you meet people, avoid talking about your problems or burnout.

•Call your counselor once while you are gone.

Jim typed this list up and sent it with me. He told me to put it in an obvious place so I would see it and read it every day. I have to admit that that vacation was the first time in my life I ever took time off just to rest and relax. It did wonders for my attitude and physical condition.

I returned home two weeks later feeling far less stress and

tension than when I had left. It seemed that my head was clearer and my problems weren't nearly as big as when I had driven out of town. I felt I was ready for the next step.

I have used this list with many others I have worked with in burnout and have seen positive results every time. If you are experiencing burnout and want to get started on the road to recovery, I highly recommend that you use it too.

BEGIN REBUILDING YOUR SELF-CONFIDENCE

Because burnout victims have developed very poor self-images, it is absolutely essential that they begin experiencing *immediate* success when they return from vacation. This is extremely important to their continued progress toward recovery. "Immediate success" is the key phrase. People don't begin rebuilding self-confidence by sitting down with a counselor, employer, or friend and drawing up five-year goals. If they are in burnout, they can't even think about achieving anything five days from now, let alone five years.

Self-confidence is restored by frequent, successful completion of short-range goals that slowly become more difficult and longer in range as time goes by. This is one of the most important keys to the successful recovery from burnout.

For example, the day I returned from my two-week trip, Jim, my counselor, called me and invited me over for dinner. After dinner Jim challenged me to a game of chess. I was reluctant to play, but finally I agreed. And I won! That evening I had no idea of the significance of that chess game. That was the first successful completion of a whole series of short-range goals that ultimately helped bring about my recovery from burnout. (I later learned that Jim let me win the game because he wanted me to experience success.)

Let me stop right here and speak to counselors and supervisors of burnout victims. You may initially have to create success for the burnout victim in much the same way Jim did by letting me win that game of chess. You need to do whatever it takes to help the burnout victim experience success.

Now back to my story. The day after the chess game Jim called me and asked to meet me for lunch. While we were waiting for the waitress to seat us, Jim asked me if I would show him how to make transparencies for use with an overhead projector. He was getting ready to conduct a sales training program and wanted to update some of his material.

I agreed to teach him how to make them, and then he asked if I would be willing to do some team teaching with him. I had tried to avoid teaching situations and speaking engagements since my battle with burnout began, but I reluctantly agreed. Next he asked me if I would be willing to conduct a management seminar for a group of realtors, if he was able to sell them on the idea. At first I told him no, but later agreed.

Before long Jim had convinced me to start rebuilding my consulting business. It didn't happen overnight or even in a matter of days. It took months of Jim encouraging me. First it was a simple chess game, then a little bigger challenge and a little greater risk. There was nothing magic about it. Jim simply worked with me on a regular weekly (and sometimes daily) basis to help me achieve a series of very short-range goals. As I relearned that I could succeed, I slowly began to rebuild my self-confidence, which had been totally shattered.

HOW TO HELP YOUR BURNED-OUT EMPLOYEES

Even though many would never admit it, employers frequently contribute to employee burnout. If you are a supervisor reading this book, I strongly encourage you to look for symptoms of burnout in your employees and be willing to help those in burnout recover.

You may say, "But I'm not a trained counselor, and I don't know what to do." If you will read this book carefully and follow the procedures it outlines, you will be amazed at how effective you can be in helping your employees overcome burnout. But I must warn you that it will require some flexibility on your part. For example, when you discover that an employee is suffering from burnout, you *must* be willing to make time available for him to get away from the job for a period of rest and relaxation. If you value the person as an employee, you should do everything in your power to see that the company pays for this time away from the job. If you think the company can't afford it, think of it this way. Burned-out employees cost their employers countless thousands of dollars each year in loss of productivity—productivity that is paid for, but never received because the employee is burned out. The company can't afford not to send burnout victims on vacation.

Next, when the employee returns from his time away, it is vital that you make provision for him to have a change in working environment. This should be in the form of a revised job description, with new and different duties and goals. The old environment helped develop the burnout, and placing him right back in it will ensure failure to recover.

Finally, if you feel that the employee needs outside counseling, require him to get it. It should not be an option. If the employee refuses, then he isn't serious about wanting to recover from burnout and he must realize that continued poor performance will put his job in jeopardy. Be willing to work with any employee experiencing burnout that wants your help and is willing to work with you in getting it, but never compromise performance standards for a burned-out employee who refuses your help. To do so is unfair to other conscientious, productive employees.

DEVELOP A CONSISTENT EXERCISE PROGRAM

Lack of consistent exercise is part of the reason for the physical exhaustion of burnout victims. In almost all instances people in burnout fail to get proper exercise. They have become aimless and hopeless individuals without the discipline necessary to exercise on a regular basis.

At the time I started burning out, I was running three miles a day, spending a lot of time hiking in the mountains around my home, and regularly playing basketball with my son. By the time I reach the depths of burnout, I hardly had enough energy to make it out of bed in the morning.

If you are serious about your commitment to recover from burnout, you will need to sit down with your counselor and develop an exercise program. It doesn't have to be a rigorous one, but it must be consistent. There are many good books on the subject of physical fitness. Take a trip to your local bookstore, and the sales clerk will be most happy to help you find one suited to your needs.

Remember that you need to build yourself up physically before you can expect any success with your emotional and mental recovery.

DEVELOP A NEW PURPOSE AND VISION FOR YOUR LIFE

People in burnout have lost their purpose in life. They do not have a vision for the future, and they have decided to give up on life in general. If they want to recover from burnout, they must define a new purpose for their lives.

Notice that I said, "a new purpose." In all probability the old purpose—the one before burnout—contributed to your burnout. It probably isn't a good idea simply to pick up where you left off. You need to reevaluate what you want to get out of life and why. You must redefine your values and identify what is really important in life.

Make sure your purpose stimulates and motivates you. It must be worthwhile and it must challenge you to action. Be careful, however, not to let it control you to the point that it drives you to the brink of burnout as it happened in the past. Working with your counselor, set new goals for every area of your life, including family, career, leisure time, and your relationship with God.

Like the other steps we have mentioned, this one is also quite difficult. People in burnout are not used to thinking in terms of purpose, vision, goals, and objectives. They have been letting life happen to them instead of actively planning their lives. Instead of controlling circumstances, they have allowed circumstances to control them. All that must change. People in burnout have to be willing to once again plot courses of action for their lives. They have to develop reasons for getting up in the morning, dressing, and walking out the door into the world outside. And as they develop their new purpose and vision, they will once again know that life is truly worth living.

QUESTIONS PEOPLE ASK ABOUT THE RECOVERY PROCESS

During seminars on burnout I am frequently asked a number of questions concerning the recovery process. Since you may be asking some of the same questions, I will answer some of the most common ones.

How long does it take to recover from burnout? The length of time will vary from person to person. However, it will generally take from several months to a year or more.

How often should I meet with my burnout counselor? At first you should be willing to meet with your counselor at least twice a week. Sometimes you may need to meet even more often than that. At some point, depending on your progress, your counselor will reduce it to once a week and then every two weeks, and so on.

For how long will my counselor and I need to meet? You will need to meet for at least six months. Exact time frames will vary from person to person.

Can one ever recover completely from burnout? Yes! In fact, if you properly replace bad habits with good habits, you can become a much more productive person than you were before burning out.

Is it possible to go through burnout again once you have recovered? Definitely. If you allow yourself to fall back into the old habits that caused burnout initially, you will experience burnout again. However, the second time around burnout will occur much more quickly. It frequently takes a person many years in a situation before they burn out for the first time. However, the second time around it can happen in a matter of months.

Also, the second time a person experiences burnout, there is a far greater possibility that he will never recover and will experience permanent emotional damage. Therefore, it is very important that the person recovering from burnout be committed to consistently applying the principles for keeping his life in balance and avoiding burnout syndrome in the future.

Is burnout becoming a bigger problem, or is it just a popular, catch-all phrase we use to describe our problems? Burnout is definitely a greater problem in our society today than in the past. There are many reasons for this, but the biggest is that people in our society are under much more pressure today than in generations past. We place great emphasis on achievement and production, and we are part of a highly competitive society. In addition, our whole economic environment is much more unstable than in the past. It is much more difficult for businesses to develop and maintain strong financial bases, yet there is a strong emphasis on business growth. People in our society are becoming increasingly less tolerant of others. This adds to the pressures already existing in the work force and makes management and supervision much more difficult than in years past. All of these factors, and others we don't have the space to mention, contribute greatly to the increase of burnout in our country today.

Does burnout affect a person's relationship with God? We will devote the next chapter to answering that question, but let me say here that there is usually just as much impact on spiritual health as on physical and emotional health.

EIGHT

THE SPIRITUAL ASPECTS OF BURNOUT

Burnout drains a person not only physically and emotionally, but also spiritually. Some of the greatest battles Christians in burnout face are spiritual battles. They are suddenly in the midst of a war with Satan for their spiritual lives.

Notice how 1 Peter 5:8 describes the devil. "Be careful—watch out for attacks from Satan, your great enemy. He prowls around like a hungry, roaring lion, looking for some victim to tear apart" (TLB). But lions don't look for just any prey. You never hear of a lion attacking a strong, mature elephant. Hungry lions look for the weak, sick, or wounded animal to attack because they are easy prey and can't put up much of a fight.

That is exactly the way Satan works. He prowls around like a hungry lion, looking for a weak, exhausted person to devour.

People in burnout make the perfect prey. They are physically and emotionally exhausted. Their self-confidence has been destroyed. They are ready to lie down and give up on life. They are just the juicy meal Satan is looking for.

SATAN WANTS YOU TO BLAME GOD

Satan's ultimate goal is to use your burnout experience to destroy your trust and faith in God, and he begins by trying to get you to blame God for all the problems you are having. Notice Moses' statement to God in Numbers 11:11 "Why pick on me, to give me the burden of a people like this?" (TLB) Moses blamed God for the mess he was in.

Look also at what Jeremiah told God during his bout with burnout: "O Lord, You deceived me when You promised me Your help" (Jer. 20:7, TLB). Like Moses, Jeremiah felt God had let him down. He believed God was to blame for the problems he was having with the people. Unfortunately, these are typical reactions from people experiencing burnout. They almost always blame God for their bad situations.

James Harmon called my office one day to talk to me about reviewing some of my insurance policies. I agreed to meet with him, and after he had made his presentation, I said, "Well, Mr. Harmon, I think you're offering me a good package, but I always make a habit of praying about such matters before I make a decision."

His face turned red and I could tell by his expression that he was getting angry. I assumed he was afraid of losing the sale, but I wasn't prepared for what happened next. Slamming his briefcase shut, he said angrily, "I didn't know anyone prayed anymore."

After an awkward silence he looked at me and said, "Would you believe I used to be a minister?" Before I could manage to answer he continued. "I pastored a church for fifteen years."

There was another long pause and I could tell he was having a hard time discussing it. But since he had brought up the subject I asked, "What happened? Why did you quit?"

"I just couldn't take it anymore." Then he told me his story. After graduating from seminary, he had joined the staff of a large church on the West Coast as one of its associate pastors, and when the senior pastor retired ten years later, he was asked to take his place. "I was very good at preparing sermons, but I was a terrible administrator. They taught me everything in seminary except how to manage. I realized one day that I didn't know how to use my staff effectively. I was doing all the work, and they were sitting on the sidelines looking on."

He frowned and said, "I knew I was doing something wrong, but I didn't know how to correct it. I was getting more and more exhausted with each passing week. It seemed my office was always full of people wanting me to do something, go somewhere, or see someone. Finally I just couldn't take it anymore. With all those people wanting to see me, I never had time to properly prepare my sermons. One day I realized I just didn't want to be there anymore. I no longer cared about those people or my sermons. I just wanted out. So I quit and started selling insurance."

James Harmon had obviously burned himself out. But I still didn't know why he was so angry; I soon found out. As James picked up his briefcase and started toward the door to leave, he looked at me and said, "You want to know why I never pray anymore? God let me down. I felt God called me to preach, not manage a large organization. It takes time to prepare good sermons, but I never had the time because of all the interruptions."

As we approached the door, James put his coat on. "I finally told God if He wouldn't give me the time I needed to prepare my sermons, I'd quit. He never answered my prayers, so I quit!"

After James Harmon left I sat down again, not believing what I had just heard. Ten years ago Satan had cleverly convinced an emotionally exhausted, burned-out pastor that it was God's fault he was so busy dealing with details that he didn't have time to properly prepare his messages. James had blamed God for the organizational problems that developed because of his own failure to properly delegate responsibilities. And ten years later he was still blaming God. In fact, Satan had used James' burnout to destroy his relationship with God. James Harmon not only blamed God for his administrative problems in the church, he had become a very angry, bitter man who never even bothered to pray anymore.

My own experience with burnout taught me how vulnerable we can become to Satan's attacks when we are physically and emotionally exhausted. I also went through a period of time when I blamed God for what had happened to me. I remember one evening sitting alone in my tiny apartment staring at my Bible and complaining to God that He had let me down. I remember thinking to myself, *Is this what I get for serving God?* I became so angry at God that I grabbed my Bible and threw it as hard as I could against the wall across the room.

Like Moses, Jeremiah, and James Harmon, I felt betrayed by God. I kept asking myself, *Why did God let me down and let this happen to me?* I was confused, and I was angry with God, even though I didn't want to admit it.

I remember driving down the freeway one day thinking, *If God couldn't keep this from happening to me, how can I ever trust Him for anything else again?* I didn't know it at the time, but I was playing right into Satan's hands. He loved it. He heartily agreed with that line of thinking and made sure I dwelled on such negative thoughts about God day after day.

As I look back, I can see that Satan was viciously attacking me, but at the time I was unaware that he was promoting those thoughts in an effort to get me to blame God for my problems and turn my back on Him. I was fortunate to have many people praying for me during those very dark days in my life. Without those prayers I'm sure I never could have recovered spiritually from the devastating attacks of Satan during my life-and-death struggle with burnout.

SPIRITUAL NUMBNESS

The spiritual exhaustion that occurs during burnout leads to spiritual numbness. While I was conducting a workshop on burnout for a group of pastors, one of them admitted, "I'm so exhausted I don't even feel like praying. And when I do pray it seems as though there is no one listening—it's like talking to the wall."

As he spoke I was reminded of David's statement in Psalm 22:1-2. "My God, my God, why have You forsaken me? Why do You refuse to help me or even to listen to my groans? Day and night I keep on weeping, crying for Your help, but there is no reply" (TLB). I could identify with both the pastor and David. I felt God was so far away that He couldn't possibly hear when I cried out for help. In my physically and emotionally exhausted condition, praying seemed an enormous chore. I remember going into a fast food restaurant one day for lunch and dozing off to sleep while trying to thank God for the hamburger, french fries, and Coke. I was so embarrassed when I woke up that I got up and left without eating my meal. Spiritual activities, such as praying or reading the Bible, frequently seem to require more strength and effort than we have during burnout.

A well-meaning and concerned friend of mine called me one day and asked, "How is your 'quiet time' these days, Myron?"

"Very quiet," I replied, trying to inject a little humor into my voice and not wanting him to think my spiritual life had gone into foreclosure. My friend spent the next fifteen minutes talking to me about how important it was for me to maintain a consistent time of prayer and Bible study during this very trying time in my life. He quoted several verses and said he was going to drop off some books he wanted me to read.

I knew he was right. But my emotional energy level was so low, it was all I could do to read a few verses from the Book of Psalms each week, let alone do a verse-by-verse study of a passage. I already felt guilty about the way my relationship with God had been eroding, and my friend's lecture only added to my feelings of failure, frustration, anger, and guilt.

GUILT TRIPS ASSOCIATED WITH SPIRITUAL BURNOUT

Christians experiencing burnout get a double dose of frustrations, feelings of failure, lose of self-confidence, and feelings of hopelessness because not only are they having serious emotional battles, they are also facing some of the greatest spiritual struggles of their lives. In a state of physical and emotional exhaustion, it is even more difficult to succeed in these struggles.

The person experiencing burnout feels that his world is collapsing around him. If he is a Christian, Satan launches a campaign to convince him that his problems are God's fault. As the Christian in burnout blames God, his relationship with his Heavenly Father is increasingly undermined. This produces enormous feelings of guilt, which start driving the person experiencing spiritual burnout even further from God.

Guilt makes us want to hide from God. Remember Adam and Eve's reaction to God when they ate the forbidden fruit in the Garden of Eden? "That evening they heard the sound of the Lord God walking in the garden; and they hid themselves among the trees" (Gen. 3:8, TLB). Adam and Eve disobeyed God, and the resulting guilt caused them to run and hide from Him. People in spiritual burnout who blame God for their situations have the same reaction. Guilt causes them to want to run and hide from God.

During my battles with burnout I developed overwhelming feelings of guilt. As a result, I also tried to run and hide from God. But how can one really hide from God?

In counseling with Christians experiencing burnout I have observed that one of the ways they try to hide from God is to withdraw from other Christians. This was also true in my case. I started turning down invitations to get together with Christian friends. I dropped out of the Bible studies I was in. I stopped attending church on a regular basis. I spent less and less time praying and studying the Bible.

As a result, I developed a serious case of spiritual apathy, and Satan loved it. In running from God, His Word, and His people, I was turning my back on the greatest source of help in my greatest time of need. I was forcing myself to try to solve my problems on my own, and in my state of exhaustion that was impossible.

Guilt causes us to feel a need for punishment. Genesis 37 describes how jealousy and hatred drove Joseph's brothers to sell him into slavery, and Genesis 42 describes how the problems they encountered trying to get food and grain in Egypt during a famine in their own country caused them to feel that they were being punished for the wrong they had committed. "Surely we are being punished because of our brother. We saw how distressed he was when he pleaded with us for his life, but we would not listen; that's why this distress has come upon us" (Gen. 42:21, NIV).

Their consciences had obviously been bothering them, and they felt guilty for selling Joseph into slavery. Their guilt led them to believe that their problems were punishment for their crimes. Their guilt caused them to feel that they deserved to be punished.

Because we feel we deserve the bad things that happen to us, if the guilt is allowed to go on, we may find ourselves subconsciously doing things to continue our punishment. In other words, we may actually wind up creating problems for ourselves because of the guilt we are carrying around on our shoulders.

THE BATTLE WITH BITTERNESS

As I mentioned earlier, Satan attempts to get Christians in burnout to blame God for their problems because blaming God eventually leads to bitterness. Bitterness can destroy both the individual and those around him like a spreading epidemic. We are warned in Scripture concerning bitterness: "Watch out that no bitterness takes root among you, for as it springs up it causes deep trouble, hurting many in their spiritual lives" (Heb. 12:15, TLB).

Bitterness has the power to destroy us spiritually. That is what happened to James Harmon, the former pastor turned insurance salesman. He had become an angry, bitter man, allowing his resentments to destroy his relationship with God. His bitterness was so strong that he even made fun of others who prayed for guidance in making decisions.

Paul, in Ephesians 4:31, tells us to "get rid of all bitterness, rage and anger, brawling and slander, along with every form of malice" (NIV). *The Living Bible* paraphrases this verse, "Stop being mean, bad-tempered and angry. Quarreling, harsh words, and dislike of others should have no place in your lives."

The person filled with bitterness is unable to get along with anyone—including himself. He is filled with rage and anger. He won't forgive himself or others for mistakes of the past. He is a troublemaker, always lashing out and accusing others instead of recognizing his own contribution to the problem.

This makes it very difficult for God to work in the person's life. He becomes hardened to the Holy Spirit's efforts to deal with his conscience. He blames God for his problems, and eventually he will start blaming others as well.

I had several meetings with James Harmon to discuss my insurance needs. I also tried to build a relationship with him, because he was a very lonely, hurting man. But James would never let me through the walls he had built around his emotions.

During one meeting with James I invited him to a Bible study, but he refused. "I've probably forgotten more about the Bible than you'll ever know!" he snapped. "And look where it got me. No thanks. I'm sure I can find something better to do with my time than meet with a bunch of misguided Christians."

I felt very sorry for James. He didn't appear to have many friends, yet when I tried to strike up a friendship with him, he was quick to let me know he wasn't interested. Yet he obviously missed the fellowship of other Christians he had once had, because during one of his less guarded and more open and relaxed moments he once said. "I still miss that feeling of 'family' we had in the church I pastored in California. You can't duplicate that in the insurance business." However, when I suggested he might find that same warm, friendly atmosphere in a local church, he said, "Myron don't start preaching at me again. You're just wasting your time."

So far James has been right. I have not been able to find a crack in his wall of bitterness. But I pray that God will help him rediscover his personal relationship with Jesus Christ.

RECOVERING FROM SPIRITUAL BURNOUT

While one is following the procedures outlined in the previous chapter for overcoming emotional burnout, there are some additional activities that are required in order to recover from spiritual burnout. In fact, applying the principles for spiritual recovery will greatly enhance the progress being made toward emotional recovery.

God promises to help us. The first step in recovering from spiritual burnout is to rely on God's power. Notice His promise in Psalm 34:7: "For the Angel of the Lord guards and rescues all who reverence Him" (TLB). What does the verse promise? It tells us that God will both *guard* us from evil and *rescue* us from our problems. Every Christian in burnout should memorize that verse.

Then notice God's great promise in Psalm 41:2-3. "He protects them and keeps them alive; He publicly honors them and destroys the power of their enemies. He nurses them when they are sick, and soothes their pains and worries" (TLB). The person in burnout has many pains and worries, but this passage promises that God is available to remove them.

In order for God to help us, we must be willing to get our eyes off ourselves and onto God. Notice what David says in Psalm 123:1-2. "O God enthroned in heaven, I lift my eyes to You. We look to Jehovah our God for His mercy and kindness just as a servant keeps his eyes upon his master or a slave girl watches her mistress for the slightest signal" (TLB). It is hard for people in burnout to get their eyes off themselves. They are usually wallowing in self-pity, feeling totally alone and deserted. They are convinced that their situations are hopeless, because it seems impossible for them to solve their problems—and it is. But once they get their eyes off themselves and onto God, they realize that He is ready and able to solve all their problems.

Be willing to ask for and accept God's forgiveness. This step has two parts. First we must be willing to ask God to forgive us for our negative and hostile feelings toward Him and others. Second, we must also be willing to accept His forgiveness. John states, "If we confess our sins to Him, He can be depended on to forgive us and to cleanse us from every wrong" (1 John 1:9, TLB).

It is easy to know that verse in our heads, but during

burnout it can be very difficult to accept it in our hearts. In order to accept God's forgiveness, we must also be willing to forgive ourselves, and as we have seen, this can be very difficult for the person in burnout.

Spiritual recovery, however, will not be possible as long as we are unwilling to forgive ourselves. A number of people in burnout have told me, "I know God forgives me, but I just can't seem to forgive myself." I must admit that I too was guilty of that same thing.

But that is a cop-out. If we really understand God's forgiveness, it is easy to forgive ourselves. That doesn't mean we will ever forget, but we know that God has. Listen to how David describes God's love and forgiveness. "He has not punished us as we deserve for all our sins, for His mercy toward those who fear and honor Him is as great as the height of the heavens above the earth. He has removed our sins as far away from us as the east is from the west. He is like a father to us, tender and sympathetic to those who reverence Him" (Psalm 103:10-13, TLB). According to this passage, God loves us as a father loves his children, and He not only forgives us, but removes our sins out of His sight as far as the east is from the west—and that's a long way!

Reopen the lines of communication with God. In order to recover from spiritual burnout, we must reopen the lines of communication with God that we severed when we started blaming Him for our problems. That means we must once again start spending time in prayer and studying His Word.

That does not mean you can pick up where you left off before burnout. Don't try to commit to thirty minutes or an hour each day of prayer and Bible study the first week. Remember, you don't need any more failures. To begin with, spend five minutes a day in prayer and read a few passages of Scripture—and don't worry if at first you can't draw a personal application from what you read.

If you have a hard time making up your mind where to start reading, try the Psalms. Remember, David also had a bout with burnout, and you will find that you will be able to relate to many of his writings in a personal way.

As time goes by you can gradually increase the amount of time you spend praying and reading each day. Keep in mind that the amount of time spent isn't nearly as important as your honesty and sincerity with God and yourself. As long as you are honest and sincere, you will have a meaningful quiet time. The length of time will increase as needed.

Begin rebuilding relationships with Christians. Serious blows and deep wounds occur to relationships during burnout. I have seen business partnerships dissolved, marriages ruined, and friendships destroyed as a result of burnout. During burnout things are said and done that can't be retracted or undone. Bad memories and resentments toward others tend to linger long after we ask God to forgive us for what we said and did. The person who wants to recover from spiritual burnout must consider Jesus' statement in Mark 11:24-25. "Listen to me! You can pray for *anything* and *if you believe, you have it*; it's yours! But when you are praying, first forgive anyone you are holding a grudge against, so that your Father in heaven will forgive you your sins too" (TLB). Jesus makes it very clear in this passage that if we expect God to forgive us and reestablish a relationship with us, we also must be willing to forgive others who have wronged us. It isn't an option.

LOVE YOURSELF AGAIN

It is impossible to fully recover from spiritual burnout until we learn to love ourselves again. You may be saying, "What do you mean, Myron? I thought Christians were to deny self, not love it." When the Bible speaks of denying self, it means putting God ahead of personal will, goals, ambitions, and desires. It means making Jesus Christ Lord and master in our lives.

That is different from the respect and love for oneself that the Bible teaches is important. Notice what Jesus says: "Love the Lord your God with all your heart, soul, and mind. This is the first and greatest commandment. The second most important is similar: Love your neighbor as much as you love yourself"

(Matt. 22:37-39, TLB). Love and respect for oneself is very important. If we can't love ourselves we certainly can't know how to love others. If we don't respect ourselves we certainly won't respect others.

People experiencing burnout lose a great deal of their self-confidence and as a result develop poor self-images. They begin to lose respect for themselves. In short, they find it hard to love themselves. This is a very serious problem, because without love and respect for oneself there isn't much reason to live. And there isn't much reason to care about others and how our actions affect them.

The absence of self-respect breeds self-contempt, and self-contempt leads to self-destruction. We must learn to love ourselves again if we expect to successfully recover from spiritual and emotional burnout. The best way to do this is to realize just how great God's love is for us.

Read the following passages, which describe just how very much God loves us.

- See how very much our Heavenly Father loves us, for He allows us to be called His children—think of it—and we really *are!* (1 John 3:1, TLB)
- But God showed His great love for us by sending Christ to die for us while we were still sinners (Rom. 5:8, TLB).
- For long ago the Lord had said to Israel: "I have loved you, O My people, with an everlasting love; with lovingkindness I have drawn you to Me" (Jer. 31:3, TLB).

Throughout history God has faithfully demonstrated His great and endless love for us. We are His prized children. He is our Heavenly Father. No matter how bad we act, He still loves us. I don't know about you, but to me that means I must be worth loving, and that realization helps me take a giant step forward in recovering from emotional and spiritual burnout.

NINE

COUNSELING BURNOUT VICTIMS

Note: This chapter is designed to show *anyone* how to counsel and help someone in burnout. You don't have to be a professional counselor to make a positive contribution to the life of the burnout victim. Even though you may not feel qualified, this chapter will give you the tools you need to help guide the person in burnout back to a normal, productive, and balanced life.

Proverbs 27:17 states, "As iron sharpens iron, so one man sharpens another" (NIV). This verse could never be more true than in the case of a counselor working with a person in burnout. The interaction, discussions, advice, and counsel exchanged between two persons help them become sharper and more productive.

When I was a small boy living on a farm in the red sand hills of central Oklahoma, it was my job every spring to go the toolshed, take the garden hoes down from the nail they had been hanging on all winter, and clean and sharpen them in preparation for planting the garden. I always liked that job. During the cold, damp winter months the hoes usually accumulated a great deal of rust. I would find the long file on the workbench, place a hoe in the vice, and slowly begin to file away its rusted edge. With each stroke of the file, fine iron shavings from the edge of the hoe would fall to the floor, and slowly the dull, rusted edge of the hoe would become shiny and sharp. If you have ever chopped weeds with a garden hoe you know that the job can be accomplished much easier and faster with a sharp hoe than with a dull, rusty one.

Counseling a person in burnout is very similar to filing a garden hoe. Burnout takes away the sharp edge of the once highly productive person. He becomes dull and rusty. The counselor serves as the file, and just as the file slowly sharpens the dull, rusted edge of a hoe, so the counselor slowly helps remove the dulling and damaging effects of burnout and helps the burned-out person become as sharp and good as new.

In this chapter we will take a close look at the counseling process. Even though the emphasis will be on the counselor, the person in burnout should not skip this chapter. The more he understands the role and purpose of the counselor, the more smoothly his recovery from burnout will go. I speak from experience.

THE ROLE OF THE BURNOUT COUNSELOR

The counselor plays a key role in the person's recovery from burnout. In all likelihood, the burnout victim will never recover without help from you or some other counselor who understands burnout and the process involved in recovery. Therefore, I encourage you to reread this book as many times as it takes for you to develop a clear understanding of the points and principles presented in each chapter. (This will be even more necessary if you have never gone through burnout personally.)

Believe that the person will recover. Remember, the person in burnout has lost faith in himself. He no longer thinks he can succeed. He sees himself as a failure and in all probability, those around him—his family and close friends—are beginning to see him in the same light. You are the catalyst for restoring his faith in himself, and without faith in oneself, there can be no recovery from burnout!

Your faith and belief in the person's ability to recover must be communicated during your first visit to discuss his burnout. Remember Bud and Kay Hillery from chapter five? The evening in the restaurant when I first discussed with them Bud's burnout I let both of them know that I knew it was possible for Bud to recover.

My objective was to instill hope in Bud and Kay because both of them felt that the situation was hopeless. Always remember: *burnout is never hopeless.* Recovery is always possible, as long as the individual is willing to follow the steps and apply the principles necessary for recovery.

Therefore, one of your major roles as counselor of the burnout victim is to communicate, "I believe in you." This belief will have to be reaffirmed continually. Every time you meet with the person in burnout or talk to him on the phone you must get across the fact that the person can and will recover.

Never give up on the burnout victim. I can't emphasize this point strongly enough. You must *never* give up on the burnout victim you are counseling. Again let me repeat: he has given up on himself, and many of those closest to him are probably in the process of giving up on him also. You may be the only person he knows who believes there is hope for him. If you give up on him too, it may be so devastating to him emotionally that he may never recover. *Even if he gives up on you and your ability to help him, don't you give up on him.*

Always be available to help. This is the ultimate proof that you really do believe that the person can recover. You aren't just giving lip service to your faith in the burnout victim; you are backing up your words with action and commitment.

Remember, God certainly isn't giving up on the person in burnout. No matter how many times a person blows it, no matter how slow the recovery process, God never says, "I've had enough! Don't ever bother to call Me again! I'm writing you off as hopeless!"

No, God is always available to help. And we, the counselors, must be also. No matter how many times they blow it, or fail to do assignments, or say, "I quit!" always be ready to help pick up the pieces once again and continue helping them through the recovery process—even if it means starting over again and again.

I can speak from experience that it pays great dividends. I quit on Jim, my counselor, many times before my recovery was complete. But thankfully he never quit on me. First Corinthians 15:58 challenges us to "stand firm. Let nothing move you. Always give yourselves fully to the work of the Lord, because you know that your labor in the Lord is not in vain" (NIV).

Be a good listener. Every good counselor has learned the importance of applying James 1:19: "Don't ever forget that it is best to listen much, speak little, and not become angry" (TLB). Good counselors are good listeners. You can't help someone unless you know what his real needs are. You must learn how he feels and why he feels that way. This can only be accomplished through effective listening.

At first you will be listening to a very negative person. He will be down on himself—and probably down on the world. He will probably complain about everything from the weather to the way the person serving the coffee fills the cup. He will tend to react negatively to most of your suggestions and assignments.

Always take good notes during your meetings. Record such things as attitudes, reactions, feelings, and especially results of assignments. This will allow you to note the progress of the burnout victim. As time goes by, look and listen for changes in attitude. As the burnout victim begins to experience success with the assignments given, you should start seeing a more positive person who is starting to regain some self-confidence. But if you fail to see progress in the person, and if he seems to be more and more depressed or begins talking about suicide, immediately refer him to a professional counselor.

You are first and foremost a friend. Keep in mind that you are first a friend and then a burnout counselor. Even though the burnout victim doesn't want to be around people, he desperately needs a friend, and he usually feels as though he doesn't have any friends left. So spend some recreational and social time with the person you are counseling. In fact, your best counseling sessions will probably occur during an evening of bowling, following a game of tennis, while sharing a day of fishing, or in some other informal setting.

Keep in mind that most people in burnout don't need to see a psychiatrist. They need someone who believes in them and can help them learn again to believe in themselves. This is best done by keeping a low "counseling" profile.

Let the person know you want to get together as a friend, and that you are interested in helping him as a friend. For example, when Jim Ander first offered to meet with me to "discuss" my burnout, I was very reluctant. I told Jim he was too busy with his business and family to worry about me too. But he wouldn't take no for an answer. He said, "Myron, a person isn't much of a friend if he isn't available when you need him."

Jim always emphasized the fact that he was available as a friend and he was concerned as a friend. By the time my recovery from burnout was completed, Jim had become the best friend a person could have.

You are a facilitator and a motivator. You are the one who facilitates change. You will have to help motivate the burnout victim to action. Remember, this former high achiever has shifted his life into neutral—maybe even reverse! As a result, he will probably not volunteer to take action on his own.

For example, people in burnout frequently develop a "savior complex" toward their counselors and rely on them to tell them step by step what to do and when to do it. You may find yourself needing to assist the burnout victim in locating a place to get away for a period of rest and relaxation. Sometimes just deciding where to go is more than the person in burnout can handle. You should be prepared to make telephone calls, gather information, and even help pack, if necessary, in order to facilitate the rest and relaxation necessary to recovery.

You will certainly need to be deeply involved in determining short-range goals that help provide "instant success." And you will need to become directly involved in helping the burnout victim establish a new purpose and new goals in every area of his life.

If you don't facilitate the development of such things, they will never get done; consequently the burnout victim will never recover from burnout. So don't make the mistake that a lot of burnout counselors make. They frequently think that their job is simply to make suggestions and steer the burnout victim in the right direction. Then they become frustrated because nothing happens. They don't realize that when dealing with burnout victims, usually nothing happens until the counselor rolls up his sleeves and gets directly involved in helping the person make the decisions.

Maintain integrity. It is very important to remember that you must maintain strict confidentiality when counseling your burnout victim. Failure to do so will undermine your integrity and destroy your credibility.

Don't discuss publicly the things the person in burnout tells you in private—not even with members of your own family. If the burnout victim wants to discuss with others how the counseling is going, that's his business. But you should never take it on yourself to share such information.

HOW TO APPROACH THE SUBJECT OF BURNOUT

It is not always easy to approach the subject of burnout with those caught in its clutches, and when you finally do, the person in burnout may be very reluctant to discuss his personal problems. Here are some things you can do to break the ice and begin discussing burnout with its victims:

- Offer an article or book on the subject of burnout. They may not read it, but it will allow you the opportunity to bring up the subject of burnout again. You can always describe the article or book to them later if they were unwilling to read it.
- Tell of your own experience with burnout (if you've had one) or tell of someone you know who has been through it.
- Frequently let them know you are available to help in any way you can, even if it is just to listen.
- Suggest getting together to discuss specifically their burnout experience and how you might help them recover.

- If you are dealing with an employee, treat this as a performance review, letting them know how his performance has been suffering and your feelings concerning the possibility that he may be experiencing burnout.

THE FIRST MEETING

The first meeting with the burnout victim should be in a relaxed atmosphere. Personally, I like to meet at a restaurant for coffee or dessert because it represents a neutral spot and offers a social, friendly setting. *Never have the first meeting in the home of the burnout victim or in your home.* This may inhibit the person, making him feel uncomfortable and unwilling to talk freely about his problems.

During this first meeting make sure you cover the following points:

- Emphasize your belief in the person's ability to overcome burnout. If you have been through burnout, *briefly* relate the highlights of your recovery.
- Recommend that the burnout victim read this book. Show him the book and tell him you will be using it as a guide and discussing with him the various points and principles presented.
- Briefly, in no more than five minutes, review the process of burnout recovery. You may want to make reference to the chapters in this book on recovery. Again, reaffirm to him that you know he will recover from burnout.
- If the person is a Christian, show him the passages in the Bible that describe Moses', Jeremiah's, or Elijah's burnout experiences. This will show that even the most godly people experience this problem.
- Frequently ask if the individual has any questions. At this first meeting it isn't necessary for him to tell his whole story as to how and why he is in burnout. This will unfold in future meetings.
- At the end of the meeting explain the importance of being accountable to the counselor. Reaffirm your own commit-

BURNOUT RECOVERY PACT
COUNSELOR'S COMMITMENT

_____, I want
name of burnout victim

you to know that as your friend I am totally committed to helping you recover from burnout in any way I can. I know you want to recover, and I know you will. You can count on me to stand by you during this very trying time in your life. You can also count on me to keep everything we discuss during our counseling sessions in strict confidence. Thanks for letting me team up with you to win your battle with burnout.

_____   _____
date   signature of counselor

BURNOUT VICTIM'S COMMITMENT

_____, I am
name of counselor

eager to have you help me overcome burnout, and I want you to know that I will make myself accountable to you for completing all the assignments we develop.

_____   _____
date   signature of burnout victim

Figure 1. Burnout recovery pact.

ment to the individual. Ask if he is willing to make a commitment of accountability to you in order for you to help him overcome burnout. Since this is often awkward for the counselor to do, we have included a sample accountability worksheet that you might want to use with the burnout victim. (See figure 1.)

- This first meeting should not take longer than an hour. Your objective is to acquaint the person with the process of recovery, let him know you have faith in his ability to recover, make a commitment to help him recover, and invite him to trust you and become accountable to you for recovery.
- If he agrees to be accountable to you, set a time to get together in the next three or four days to get started.
- Either give or lend him a copy of this book and ask him to have the first four chapters read by the next meeting date.

THE SECOND MEETING

The night before your second meeting call the burnout victim to make sure he is still planning to meet you the next day at the agreed-upon time and location. Remember that it is not unlikely that he has forgotten or changed his mind about the meeting. This meeting should take no longer than an hour and a half. During this second meeting cover the following points:

- Ask if he read the first four chapters of this book. If he has, congratulate him for completing his first assignment and reaffirm your faith in him. If he has not, remind him of the burnout recovery pact you both signed and explain again that it will be impossible for you to help him unless both of you comply with that agreement.
- Give him his copy of the signed burnout recovery pact worksheet. (You will need to have a copy made for him before this meeting.)
- Have him begin telling you about the things he feels have contributed and are contributing to his burnout. Be sure to take good notes during this discussion, since this infor-

mation will be used in future sessions.

* Make sure he understands what burnout is. Go over the definition with him and assure him that he is not experiencing some disturbing mental illness.
* Begin discussing the factors that have led to the buildup of emotional, physical, and spiritual exhaustion in his life.
* Have him evaluate his spiritual condition.
* Find out how his family is reacting to his burnout and, if he is married, ask if he would mind bringing his spouse to a future meeting if necessary.
* Ask him to read the rest of the book by the time you meet again.
* Tell him to read chapters 5–7 very carefully and be prepared to start planning for some time away for rest and relaxation. Tell him to give special attention to the section in chapter 6 regarding this time of vacation.
* If your friend is married, set up a time during the week when you can meet with the burnout victim's spouse for coffee or dessert. Use this time to assure him or her that you feel the person you are counseling will recover from burnout. Also try to evaluate the impact his burnout is having on the family.
* Set a time for the third counseling session in about one week.

PLANNING FOR REST AND RELAXATION

Planning the time of rest and relaxation is the first major step in launching the recovery process. The third meeting is designed to begin laying those plans. During this meeting ask the burnout victim his response to chapters 5–7 and discuss the important points.

Next zero in on the section about the time of rest and relaxation in chapter 6 and study closely the list of do's and don'ts given there. Go over that list item by item and get a commitment from the person in burnout to agree to apply the list and follow its instructions.

Next you will need to decide how much time can be allotted for this period of rest and relaxation. Keep in mind that

REST AND RELAXATION WORKSHEET

1. Where do you plan to go for rest and relaxation?

   _____

   When?_____
2. What type of recreation do you plan to be involved in? _____
3. What new sport or activity do you plan to try?

   _____
4. What reading material will you take with you?

   _____
5. Who is going with you?

   _____

DO'S AND DON'TS

A. Don't try to evaluate yourself or solve problems.
B. Don't take any work with you from your job and don't call the office.
C. Do something different each day. Have fun and relax!
D. Avoid discussing your burnout.
E. Read something from the Bible each day.
F. Call your counselor once while you are gone (if your trip will last several days).
G. If the whole family is going, make it a fun trip for everyone.

Figure 2. Rest and relaxation worksheet.

you will have to be flexible in this area. Ideally, the burnout victim should have a couple of weeks away from the source of the burnout. However, his schedule may not allow for that much time. You may have to settle for several weekends away or a day once a week. All of this must be discussed in detail with the burnout victim and decisions made as to how and when the needed rest will occur.

Once this is decided, take time to discuss where the burnout victim will go for this time of rest. It might be a cabin in the hills, a resort, or a a friend's house. Again each burnout victim's circumstances will affect these decisions, but do try to stay as close as possible to the recommendations I have already made.

Always keep in mind that you will probably need to be directly involved in helping the burnout victim make these decisions. The sample rest and relaxation worksheet shown in figure 2 may be used as a guide for helping the burnout victim make these decisions.

DEVELOPING A PHYSICAL FITNESS PROGRAM

Keep in mind that the burnout victim must begin to rebuild his physical strength before he is ready to start recovering emotionally. As soon as he returns from a time of relaxation, meet together to develop a physical fitness program.

This does not need to be an elaborate program designed to prepare the person in burnout for Olympic competition. Its purpose is to improve overall body fitness through some type of regular exercise. Physical exercise is a great release for the tension and stress that build up during burnout, and it is this tension and stress that wear the body down.

Depending on the burnout victim's interests and abilities, there is a wide range of activities he or she can participate in for exercise, such as running, swimming, aerobics, hiking, weight lifting, playing tennis or handball, and many others. During your meeting discuss the various options with the person in burnout and use the physical exercise worksheet shown in figure 3 to help him decide on his exercise program. The burnout

PHYSICAL EXERCISE WORKSHEET

1. Describe the types of physical activities you plan to be involved in as a part of your physical exercise program.

   _____

   _____

   _____

   _____

2. List the activity you plan to do each day and the time you plan to do it.

Day	Activity	Time
Sunday		
Monday		
Tuesday		
Wednesday		
Thursday		
Friday		
Saturday		

Figure 3. Physical exercise program.

victim should have a physical checkup and his doctor should approve the physical fitness program before it is implemented.

Be prepared to participate with the burnout victim occasionally in order to get him started in the program. Let him know you have faith in his ability to consistently follow the schedule and be sure to give him proper recognition for a job well done. This is very important in rebuilding his self-confidence.

HELPING REBUILD SELF-CONFIDENCE

You will need to help the person in burnout develop very short-range goals that can be successfully completed, goals that can be accomplished in one day. Keep in mind the person in burnout needs immediate success. As the burnout victim begins to experience success, the goals should become longer in range and more difficult.

It is very important for you, the counselor, to follow up immediately on the burnout victim's short-range goals. For example, if he plans to clean the garage one day, call that night to ask how it went and if the job has been completed. However, don't make your calls sound like "big brother" checking up to make sure a job was done; call as a friend interested in how the day went. Always encourage the person in burnout, regardless of the amount of progress made. Even if he failed to start on the garage as planned, encourage him to do it tomorrow.

Never be critical when the burnout victim falls short of completing a goal. He will be hard enough on himself. You should always encourage him for the amount accomplished, but also let him know you have faith in his ability to do more.

During your meeting to discuss short-range goals use the worksheet shown in figure 4. As the burnout victim becomes proficient in accomplishing short-range goals, begin lengthening the goals and use the long-range goals worksheet shown in figure 5. Long-range goals may take from one week to one year to accomplish. Goals taking a considerable length of time should be reviewed periodically to see how progress is being made.

SHORT-RANGE GOALS WORKSHEET

Day	Short-range goal
Sunday	
Monday	
Tuesday	
Wednesday	
Thursday	
Friday	
Saturday	

Figure 4. Short-range goals worksheet.

LONG-RANGE GOALS WORKSHEET

1. Write out goal stating specifically *what* and *how much* will be accomplished.

   _____

   _____

   _____

   _____

   _____

2. Give date goal is to be completed.

   _____

3. This space is for evaluating progress being made toward accomplishing the goal.

   _____

   _____

   _____

   _____

   _____

   _____

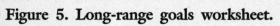

Figure 5. Long-range goals worksheet.

Short- and long-range goals must be set for every area of the person's life, including job, family, leisure, and spiritual renewal.

DEVELOPING A NEW PURPOSE

Have the person in burnout read the section on developing a new purpose and vision for life in chapter 6 and discuss it with him. Then have the burnout victim write down a new purpose statement for his life. Keep in mind that purpose tells *why* but not *how* or *when*. Purpose represents one's cause or mission in life. Once the burnout victim has completed his purpose statement, begin working with him to develop short- and long-range goals that will help him accomplish his new purpose.

WORKING TOWARD SPIRITUAL RECOVERY

Have the person in burnout read chapter 7 in this book, then meet together to discuss the chapter point by point and evaluate with him his own spiritual condition.

Using the short-range and long-range goals worksheets in figures 4 and 5, help the burnout victim set goals for his own spiritual renewal. You could go to a Christian bookstore or your pastor to seek advice on how best to help the person recover spiritually. They will be able to recommend reading and Bible study material best suited to the needs of the person in burnout.

Suggest that the burnout victim start attending a local Bible study group. He needs to reestablish contact and relationships with Christians. Also strongly encourage him to start attending church again if he has dropped out.

THE GOAL: KEEPING LIFE IN BALANCE

Your job is not only to help the person out of burnout but also to assist him in developing and keeping balance in his life. As he begins to recover from burnout, there will be a tendency for him to revert back to the old gung-ho habits that helped bring about burnout in the first place. Your job is to help ensure that he doesn't fall back into those old habits. Remember, your role is to help him unlearn those old, bad habits and replace them with some new, good ones that will bring balance to all areas of his life. You may find yourself working with the burnout victim for several months in order to accomplish this, but it will be one of the most rewarding experiences of your life.

One final word of caution—don't try to make the person you are counseling fit some other burnout victim's mold. He is a unique person. The road he traveled in reaching burnout was his own. Therefore, recognize him for the individual he is: that special, unique person unlike any other God has created. You will find that what works well with one person may not work so well with another. Each person must be allowed to recover at his own pace given his unique skills and circumstances.

Just as I know your friend can recover from burnout, I also know that you can be the counselor he needs to assist in that recovery.

Note: A packet of tools for counseling burnout victims is available from Management Training Systems. The packet includes an exclusive interview on cassette tape with my burnout counselor, Jim Ander, discussing proven techniques for counseling even the most difficult victims of burnout. This 50-minute tape also presents important do's and don'ts for dealing with varying degrees of burnout and explains the major keys for helping a person avoid burnout in the future. You will receive copies of the forms and worksheets shown in this chapter, and an expanded version of the burnout worksheet from chapter 1. To order your packet write Management Training Systems, P.O. Box 4779, Woodland Park, CO 80863 or call (303) 635-1399.

TEN

REBUILDING A POSITIVE ATTITUDE

As we have pointed out in previous chapters, high achievers generally maintain very positive attitudes. Their ability to maintain positive attitudes—even in the midst of failures—has been one of the major keys to their achievements and successes in life. But burnout changes all of this. During burnout the once-positive person becomes a negative thinker. Therefore, an important part of burnout recovery involves rebuilding positive attitudes toward self, others, God, and life in general.

THE IMPORTANT ROLE OF ATTITUDE

One of the first steps toward rebuilding a positive attitude is to recognize the important role attitudes play in life. According to Proverbs 15:15, "when a man is gloomy, everything seems to go wrong; when he is cheerful, everything seems right!" (TLB) Negative attitudes tend to produce negative results; positive attitudes tend to produce positive results.

Proverbs 23:7 seems to emphasize this point when it points out that as a person "thinketh in his heart, so is he" (KJV). Later in Proverbs we are told that "as in water face answers to face, so the mind of man reflects the man" (27:19, RSV).

All of these verses seem to be saying the same thing: our

125

attitudes play a very important role in determining what we do and accomplish in life! *Attitude* is far more important than *aptitude* when it comes to determining one's *altitude* in life.

Your attitude is one of your most important possessions. It will work either for you or against you. It will help you overcome the greatest obstacles, or it will drag you down into the very depths of despair. Attitude is to people what a rudder is to a ship—one determines the course of life while the other determines the course of the vessel. On the sea of life a positive attitude can see us through even the most violent storms and bring us safely into the harbor of success.

YOU CONTROL YOUR ATTITUDE

I generally maintained a very positive attitude before my experience with burnout, but during burnout my attitude became very negative. I developed countless reasons and excuses for why everything was falling apart in my life.

During the early stages of my recovery from burnout I gave Jim, my counselor, lots of reasons why I would fail every assignment he gave me. My attitude was, *It won't work, so why try,* and with that attitude, it usually didn't work.

One day Jim took me for a ride up in the mountains west of Colorado Springs. As we drove through the beautiful scenery around snow-covered Pikes Peak, Jim said, "You know, Myron, you have a very important decision to make if you expect to recover from burnout."

He looked at me and smiled as if to say, *Are you ready for this one?* and then continued. "You have to decide to change your attitude."

Jim spent the next half hour lecturing me about my negative attitude and how it was keeping me from recovering from burnout. He pointed out that we have control over our attitudes, and said, "Before your burnout experience you were a very positive person because you *decided* to be positive, even when confronted with a problem."

I had to agree that he was right. Then he said, "You now

have a very negative attitude because you have *decided* to think negatively when things go wrong." Jim explained that I must decide to change my attitude from negative to positive in order to accomplish the assignments he gave me and escape from burnout.

That day I discovered that *attitude is a decision.* I can decide to think positively or negatively—the choice is up to me! I am in control of my attitude because I decide how I will think, act, and react in every situation in life.

The person in burnout tends to think that the "light at the end of the tunnel" is a fast-moving train about to run over him. But even burnout can produce positive results if we let it. The choice is up to us.

Christians are never justified in thinking negatively. Notice what Romans 8:28 tells us: "In all things God works for the good of those who love Him, who have been called according to His purpose" (NIV). No matter what happens—in each set of events—God will work the situation out for our good. Realizing the truth of that great promise should make it easier for us to decide to think positively instead of negatively.

I can speak from experience that it is not easy for the person in burnout to decide to have a positive attitude. Because people in burnout tend to be controlled by emotions, and their feelings are usually negative, they tend to think negatively. But we do not have to let our feelings control us. Bad situations are never justification for negative attitudes. James writes, "Dear brothers, is your life full of difficulties and temptations? Then be happy, for when the way is rough, your patience has a chance to grow. So let it grow, and don't try to squirm out of your problems. For when your patience is finally in full bloom, then you will be ready for anything, strong in character, full and complete" (James 1:2-4, TLB). What a great passage concerning attitudes! The passage clearly tells us that a life "full of difficulties" is no excuse for a negative attitude. Even during rough times we should decide to "be happy" because we know God will use the bad experiences in life to make us strong and complete.

Attitude truly is a decision. You may not always be able to

control your circumstances, but you can certainly control how you react to them. You decide the kind of attitude you will have in each situation you face. No matter how bad your situation becomes during burnout, as James 1:2-4 points out, it is possible (and necessary) to decide to maintain a positive attitude.

WHERE TO FOCUS YOUR THOUGHTS

It isn't enough to just decide to have a positive attitude. We must focus our thoughts on things that are positive. A positive attitude will be the result. Listen to Paul's words in Philippians 4:8: "And now, brothers, as I close this letter let me say this one more thing: Fix your thoughts on what is true and good and right. Think about things that are pure and lovely, and dwell on the fine, good things in others. Think about all you can praise God for and be glad about" (TLB). This verse gives us the principles for developing and maintaining a positive attitude. Let's look at it point by point.

"Fix your thoughts." This is an important part of developing a positive attitude. We must "fix our thoughts," that is, deliberately and consciously work at focusing on the positive things in a situation instead of on the negative things.

During burnout there is ample opportunity to focus on the negative. There are frequent disappointments with oneself and others. Personal productivity is declining; goals are no longer being met. The burned-out person is losing faith in himself and feels that there are no solutions to the ever-increasing problems he faces each day. He is constantly bombarded with negative situations, thoughts, and feelings.

We must become committed to focusing on the positive even when we are being smothered with negative feelings. We must force our attention onto things that are good instead of bad, or we will never recover from burnout.

"What is true and good and right." During burnout it is hard to sort out truth from fiction. Reality becomes distorted. We tend to make mountains out of molehills. Frequently we make decisions based on assumptions and feelings instead of on facts.

Truth is never negative. Truth always leads to the positive. That is why we are challenged to fix our thoughts on what is true.

We are also told to fix our thoughts on what is "good." As we have already mentioned, the person in burnout is surrounded by bad experiences and feelings. This is why he has a negative attitude. In order to cultivate a positive attitude, we must focus on or fix our thoughts on what is good. We must look until we find the good in the situation. That is why it is so important for the person in burnout to focus his attention on such Scripture passages as Romans 8:28 and James 1:2-4. These verses remind us that there is always reason to look at the positive side of things because things are going to be better and we are going to be better persons for the experiences we are going through now.

Finally, we are to fix our thoughts on what is "right." Again, this is very difficult for people in burnout because they are operating on feeling and emotion rather than on what is right. In fact, they usually don't really know what is right, since they have lost contact with reality in most situations. But things that are true, good, and right always promote a positive attitude.

"Think about things that are pure and lovely, and dwell on the fine, good things in others." People in burnout have not only lost faith in themselves, they have also lost faith in others. They feel as though their friends are deserting them, and they have withdrawn from people. In fact, they resent others and tend to blame others for their problems because recent experiences with people have most often been negative. But negative thoughts feed negative attitudes, and the more we focus on how others have wronged us or deserted us in our time of need, the stronger our negative attitudes become.

That is why Philippians 4:8 tells us to "dwell on the fine, good things in others." As we focus on the good in others, we begin to regain faith in ourselves and those around us. Such faith is very important to the development of a strong, positive mental attitude.

"Think about all you can praise God for and be glad about." This is the most important part of the verse. Learning to know and

understand who God is and how great is His love for us is the real basis for a positive attitude. The more we focus on God and His greatness and love for us, the easier it is to think positively.

GOD IS THE SOURCE OF POSITIVE ATTITUDES

High achievers have great faith in their ability to overcome problems, meet deadlines, and accomplish goals. In fact, it was faith in their abilities that contributed to their burnout. When rebuilding a positive attitude during burnout recovery, it is important to avoid falling back into the old patterns and habits that led to burnout in the first place.

During burnout recovery God must become the source of our positive attitudes, not ourselves and our ability to produce. We must learn to let God work through us instead of always feeling that we must be working for God. We must focus on the power of God's resources instead of on the strength of our resourcefulness.

For us who are Christians, understanding the amount of power God makes available to us to accomplish His plans through us is the source of our positive attitudes. We learn to say with Paul in Philippians 4:13, "For I can do everything God asks me to with the help of Christ who gives me the strength and power" (TLB). Before burnout the high-achieving Christian was tempted to think, *I will do everything Christ asks me to if it kills me!*

Notice the amount of power that God promises is available to Christians: "Now glory be to God who by His mighty power at work within us is able to do far more than we would ever dare to ask or even dream of—infinitely beyond our highest prayers, desires, thoughts, or hopes" (Eph. 3:20, TLB). Wow! Did you grasp how much power God makes available to His people? That should spark positive thinking in all of us. God has unlimited power available to us. Our job is to allow Him the opportunity to use it through us. It may be hard for high achievers to accept, but God does not need our measly strength to accomplish His plans. All He needs is for us to let Him demonstrate and use His power through us.

I don't know about you, but my problems start looking awfully small when I start realizing how much power God has to solve them. And that is the real reason for positive thinking! When I realize that "I can do everything God asks me to with the help of Christ who gives me the strength and power" (Phil. 4:13, TLB), I have good reason to think positively.

A NEW PURPOSE

All we can do is talk philosophically about God's power available to us and the positive attitude it promotes unless that power and positive attitude are directed toward a focal point. That focal point should be the reestablishment of a purpose in life.

God had a plan for our lives before burnout (Jer. 29:11), and He also has a plan for our lives following burnout. However, as long as we are wallowing in negative thinking, it will be very difficult for us to reestablish a meaningful purpose in life that does justice to how God wants to use His mighty power in and through us to accomplish His great plans for us.

Satan is well aware of that fact, and he tries to keep us bound in the chains of negative thinking. So keep in mind that if you allow yourself to be controlled by a negative attitude, you are playing right into Satan's hands and missing God's great purpose and plan for your life.

As you decide to think positively about your new purpose in life, study carefully Jeremiah 29:11. " 'For I know the plans I have for you,' declares the Lord, 'plans to prosper you and not to harm you, plans to give you hope and a future' " (NIV). God makes it very clear that He wants to prosper us and not harm us. He has a very positive future in store for us if we choose to follow His purpose and plan for our lives.

Even though God has a different plan and purpose for each person, it always fits into His overall plan and purpose for the world. Jesus Christ said, "Come, follow Me . . . and I will make you fishers of men" (Matt. 4:19, NIV). If we are going to follow Jesus, we will be fishing for people's souls. He also tells us, "The thief's purpose is to steal, kill and destroy. My purpose is to give life in all its fullness" (John 10:10, TLB). Since God's purpose is people, any purpose we as Christians develop will include reaching people for God so they may experience "life in all its fullness."

Just as Christ took an uneducated fisherman two thousand years ago and used him to become one of the founders of the early church (Matt. 16:13-19), so today He wants to take you and me and use us to accomplish great things for Him.

MAINTAINING A POSITIVE ATTITUDE

Once we rebuild our positive attitudes, we must make sure we properly maintain them. In order to protect our positive attitudes and keep them from deteriorating into negative ones, we need to know how our conscious and subconscious minds work.

Scientists who study the mind tell us it is divided into two parts—the conscious and subconscious. The mind has been compared to an iceberg. The bulk of an iceberg lies unseen under the surface of the water with only about 10 percent of its mass visible. Likewise, it is thought that the conscious mind represents only about 10 percent of the total mind, the remaining 90 percent being made up of the subconscious.

The subconscious mind is like a giant computer. It stores, categorizes, and files both positive and negative experiences and can feed information to the conscious mind as required. It is believed that every thought, feeling, emotion, and experience of life is neatly filed away in the subconscious mind and often influences our conscious thoughts, actions, and reactions without our even being aware of it.

Therefore, it is important to guard what goes into our minds. What goes in becomes the data base from which our conscious mind draws information for decision making. If we are continually filling our minds with negative thoughts, we will tend to make negative decisions.

That is why the Bible commands us to "fix our thoughts" on things that are positive rather than negative. By filling our minds with positive thoughts, we are able to develop and maintain positive attitudes and as a result make positive decisions and have positive experiences.

Filling our minds with God's Word is one of the best ways to develop and maintain a positive attitude. Notice what the Lord tells Joshua about His Word: "Do not let this Book of the Law depart from your mouth; meditate on it day and night, so that you may be careful to do everything written in it. Then you will be prosperous and successful" (Josh. 1:8, NIV). This verse tells us that the way to positive and rewarding experiences is through filling our minds with God's Word and then making sure that we think about what God says every day. Paul describes God's Word this way: "All Scripture is God-breathed and is useful for teaching, rebuking, correcting and training in righteousness, so that the man of God may be thoroughly equipped for every good work" (2 Tim. 3:16-17, NIV). God's Word is useful for training us in righteousness and equipping us for every good work. It tells us that the Word of God prepares us for the most positive experiences in life. Therefore, you and I must focus on God's Word, fill our minds with it, and meditate on it daily, because it helps develop and maintain the proper positive attitudes necessary for experiencing a truly positive, productive, and rewarding life.

I know of no better way to rebuild a positive mental attitude than to saturate my mind with God's Word, meditate on it daily, claim its promises, and then act on its directives. The Bible is the best textbook ever written on how to live life to its fullest. It not only provides us with the way to have eternal life, it also teaches us the keys to experiencing the abundant life starting today.

Its pages are filled with instructions and principles for positive living. It shows us how to avoid negative experiences, and it teaches us how to allow God to work His mighty power in and through us, enabling us to accomplish "far more than we would ever dare to ask or even dream of—infinitely beyond our highest prayers, desires, thoughts, or hopes" (Eph. 3:20, TLB).

I challenge you to begin studying and applying God's

Word in your life on a daily basis. Then you will discover not only power for positive thinking, but the true source of power for positive living.

ELEVEN

AVOIDING BURNOUT

Recently I had the privilege of conducting a workshop on burnout with thirty couples from various mission fields. All of the couples were on furlough, and they ranged in age from the late twenties to early sixties. Nine different mission organizations were represented at this one-day seminar.

During the lunch break I sat at a table with three couples and was quickly educated concerning the life of a missionary on furlough. One couple had spent almost thirty years on the mission field. "This is our seventh furlough," they said, as they introduced themselves to the other couples. They had been back in the States seven months, traveling to meet with their various supporters and speaking in churches and to small groups explaining what life was like as a missionary in Indonesia.

As the couples got better acquainted, they began to compare notes and experiences both from their missions work and furlough time back in America. All three couples had one thing in common—they were exhausted from the continuous travel, meetings, speaking engagements, sleeping in strange beds, packing and unpacking the car as they went from trip to trip, and trying to readjust to the fast pace of life in the United States.

One woman voiced the feeling of the whole group when she said, "We spend four years overseas totally involved in the ministry of the mission, then we come back to the States for a year and spend the entire time traveling around from place to place and group to group trying to explain what we have done since we were here last. By the time we're ready to return to the field, we're more exhausted than when we arrived."

Another commented, "They tell us we're supposed to take time to rest while we're here, but there is so much to do in such a short time, you feel guilty if you even take one weekend off."

Periodically one of the missionaries would turn to me and apologize, saying, "I hope you don't lose faith in missionaries. We don't mean to complain. We love the Lord and His work, but it seems we're wearing ourselves out."

That was a very true statement. During the course of the day I discovered that most of the missionaries there were experiencing the same type of schedule I had heard described during lunch, and they also were voicing the same concerns. The majority of their lives were out of balance. They had little, if any, time for themselves and their families; they took very little time off from the ministry, even when they were on furlough; they had maintained such a full and busy schedule for so many years that they didn't know how to relax; and they felt guilty if they even thought about taking a vacation. Most of the people in that group were well on the road to burnout because their lives were out of balance. Their lives revolved around their work and ministry. As a result, the other areas of their lives, including their families, were suffering.

In this chapter we will look at principles for avoiding burnout. You *can* avoid burnout—if you apply these principles. And if you are already in burnout, these principles will ensure that you never have to worry about going through it again. These principles are designed to bring balance into your life. A balanced lifestyle is the key to avoiding burnout.

RESPECT YOUR LIMITATIONS

One of the first steps toward bringing your life into balance is to know and respect your limitations. It may come as a shock, but there are limits to what each of us can do and for how long we can do it, whether we are willing to admit it or not.

Most of the missionaries I met at the burnout workshop were pushing themselves beyond their limits, and they were paying a very high physical and emotional price for it. Dedicated Christian leaders, more than any other group, tend to push themselves too hard and too far. Like the missionaries at the lunch table, they frequently feel guilty if they take time off or slow down to rest.

The great evangelist Dwight L. Moody is a classic example of a high-achieving Christian leader who regularly pushed himself past his physical and emotional limits. Even when his doctors tried to get Moody to slow down, he refused. He was so committed to spreading the Gospel that he eventually drove himself into his grave because his body couldn't stand up under the rigorous pace. Some might think it is a mark of spiritual maturity to push that hard doing the work of the ministry. However, I believe it is a lack of respect for one's personal limitations, and it usually causes highly productive people to have their very successful ministries cut short.

Even Jesus Christ knew His human limitations and worked within them. Notice the following verses:

- "He went up into the hills by Himself to pray. When evening came, He was there alone" (Matt. 14:23, NIV).
- "Jesus left there and went along the Sea of Galilee. Then He went up into the hills and sat down" (Matt. 15:29, NIV).
- "Then, because so many people were coming and going that they did not even have a chance to eat, He said to them, 'Come with Me by yourselves to a quiet place and get some rest'" (Mark 6:31, NIV).

The Lord Jesus had a very busy schedule. He had tremendous pressures on Him from all sides. He carried the weight of the world on His shoulders. He was continually being asked to heal the sick, feed the hungry, comfort the hurting, and deal with the political and spiritual leaders of His day. Yet He regularly took time out of His busy schedule to rest and be alone because He knew His physical and emotional limitations. If

Jesus Christ recognized the importance of working within physical and emotional limitations, shouldn't we do the same?

KEEP YOUR WORK IN PERSPECTIVE

Jesus not only knew His limitations, He also kept His work in proper perspective. For three years Jesus' ministry was people. He went out of His way to meet the needs of the poor, sick, and hurting multitudes, and yet His work never possessed Him. He was never driven to try to meet every need of every person He came in contact with.

As He went from place to place preaching and performing miracles, He never attempted to be all things to all people. In Mark 1:32-35 we see Jesus healing many people and casting out demons. However, early the next morning He slipped away in the dark to a solitary place to be alone and pray. When the disciples found Him, they pointed out that everyone in the city was looking for Him. Notice Jesus' reply: "Let us go somewhere else—to the nearby villages—so I can preach there also. That is why I have come" (v. 38, NIV).

This passage teaches us that Jesus kept His work in perspective. He was able to walk away from the needs of people, even when they were clamoring for His attention. He stayed in control of His work—it never controlled Him.

In order to maintain balance in our lives we must learn from Jesus' example and keep our work in perspective. There is always plenty of work to do. As Jesus so aptly stated, "The poor you will always have with you" (Matt. 26:11, NIV). When Jesus ascended into heaven to sit at the right hand of the Father, He left multitudes behind that needed to be healed, freed from demons, and so on. Yet Jesus could pray to the Father, "I have brought You glory on earth by completing the work You gave Me to do" (John 17:4, NIV).

Jesus never experienced burnout because He knew the importance of keeping His life in balance. One of the ways He accomplished this was to keep a proper perspective on His work. Unfortunately, many Christian leaders have yet to learn that very important principle. Like my missionary friends that day at lunch, they too feel guilty if they walk away from their very important jobs in the ministry to rest, relax, or play. Likewise, some businesspeople feel they just can't afford to take time away from the business. To such people let me say that it is impossible to maintain balance in your life and avoid burnout unless you learn to keep your work in perspective as Jesus did.

THE 80/20 RULE

The 80/20 rule states that 80 percent of your success comes from 20 percent of your activity, and the remaining 80 percent of your activity produces the remaining 20 percent of your success. This rule applies to all of life. For example, studies show that for a businessperson about 20 percent of your time produces the large majority of the results. The rest of the time is taken up with routine activities that probably could and should be done by someone else. Studies reveal that in sales 20 percent of the sales force produces 80 percent of the sales volume and that 20 percent of the automobile manufacturers produce 80 percent of the cars on the road today.

The principle applies to you as well—80 percent of your success in anything you do comes from just a few really important decisions you make and a few hours you spend each day being productive. That means that a great deal of the time, energy, and effort you expend each day is going to produce only a small percentage of your success and accomplishments in life. So in order to keep your life in balance, you need to focus on minimizing or eliminating the many activities in your day that take up so much of your time yet produce such a small part of your overall results.

If you think you don't have time to spend with your family, begin to eliminate the activities you are involved in each week that are actually contributing very little to your overall productivity. You can find plenty of time for your family and still get all of the important things done as well.

You may not think you have time to get away and relax,

but you do. Start eliminating some of the activities that are part of the 80 percent that produces the mere 20 percent of your productivity, and you will find plenty of time to take a vacation.

To bring your life into balance, you need to focus on the few really important things in each area of your life because they provide most of the results; at the same time eliminate the majority of your activities and functions, which contribute so little to your life. As you do this, you will discover that you have plenty of time to devote to all of the important things in your life and still operate at a high level of productivity.

REEVALUATE GOALS AND PRIORITIES REGULARLY

The world around us is constantly changing, and we must constantly change. In fact, it is impossible to keep our lives in balance unless we make regular changes in our lives.

It took me a long time and a severe case of burnout to learn this very important principle. When I first got married, I got very involved in building a successful career so I could properly provide for my future family. I worked hard and experienced a considerable amount of success.

As we had children and my family grew, I didn't think to stop to reevaluate my priorities. I kept right on working 60–70 hours a week. I started businesses and watched them grow, then I would start another project or business.

As my family was growing up, I failed to realize that I should be spending less time with my businesses and more time with them. Finally one day my daughter wrote me a note and asked to set up a meeting with me in order to talk to me.

My world had changed, but my priorities had not. I was plugging away at building financial security for my family, but they needed my personal time as well. My priorities were out of balance, so my life was out of balance.

On a regular basis (I suggest every six months), take a day off and go somewhere by yourself to reevaluate your purpose and goals in life. Look at where you are compared to where you would like to be in accomplishing your goals. Evaluate how you are spending your time in each area of your life. Take a notepad with you and write down any changes in your life or schedule that need to be made. Spend time in prayer, asking God for direction and guidance. Use this time to reflect on life in general, and specifically evaluate whether or not you need to make changes in your priorities, purpose, and goals.

Keep in mind the need to keep a good balance in your life. It is impossible to do that unless you stop long enough from time to time to determine if you are getting out of balance. Such evaluations can't be properly conducted sitting behind the desk at work answering the phone, meeting appointments, handling correspondence, or dealing with any of the many issues you are confronted with each day.

You must get away from the daily routine of life to profitably conduct such an evaluation. It may cost you $50–$100 twice a year to get out of town for a day or two to reevaluate your purpose, goals, and priorities, but that's a small price to pay compared to the enormous cost to you physically, emotionally, and spiritually if you burn out because you didn't take the time or spend the money to conduct such an evaluation. I know—I had to go through burnout to learn the importance of this exercise.

TAKE TIME TO EXPERIENCE LIFE

Most high achievers fail to take time to really experience life. They are so busy traveling toward their goals that they forget to enjoy the trip.

In order to keep balance in your life, learn to "smell the roses along the way." For example, before my burnout experience I set goals for everything I did. I once took my family on a ten-day trip. We traveled four thousand miles in those ten days. From the time I pulled out of the driveway I was thinking about getting back.

We traveled through some of the most beautiful country in America, but my family didn't get to enjoy it. When we went through Yellowstone Park, I was in such a hurry to get going again that we didn't stay to see Old Faithful erupt because we would have had to stand around for a half hour waiting for it to blow its hot steam, water, and gases into the air.

Last year, though, I went back to Yellowstone and spent three days in the park. I watched Old Faithful erupt several times and walked as many of the trails as I wanted to. I spent two hours photographing ground squirrels as they played in the woods and gathered nuts. I drove out of my way to see parts of the park I had never seen before—I took time to "smell the roses" and live life. I lay on my back in the grass and watched the beautiful white puffs of clouds change shape against the most beautiful and breathtaking blue sky you can imagine. I'm only sorry I had to go through a burnout experience in order to learn to experience life!

How long has it been since you took a day to play in the yard; went for a hike in the woods; spent a half hour eating an ice cream cone; went out to eat without leaving a message as to where you could be reached; or took your mate to a nice hotel for a weekend and lay in the hot tub, ordered a nice meal for two, and assured that special person of his or her importance to you? If you want to keep balance in your life and avoid burnout, learn to take time to experience living! It sometimes comes as a shock to the high achiever, but there is more to life than meeting deadlines and accomplishing goals.

CULTIVATE MEANINGFUL LEISURE TIME

Many high achievers do not know how to play. High achievers usually do know how to work, and they frequently spend a great deal of time working at accomplishing goals—and they enjoy it.

A couple approached me during a coffee break at a seminar arguing about the husband's interest in his work. "I'll never experience burnout," he was saying, "because I enjoy my work."

His wife tried to point out that all he did was work and that his life was very much out of balance. In an attempt to get me to agree with him, he looked at me and asked, "There's nothing wrong with spending a lot of time at the office if you really enjoy your job, is there?"

Most high achievers *enjoy* working at their jobs or whatever activities they are involved in. They are usually very enthusiastic about what they are doing. Frequently it is their enthusiasm that causes them to expend all their emotional and physical energy, and they end up in burnout.

Unfortunately very few high achievers know how to be as creative and enthusiastic when it comes to play. In order to maintain balance in our lives, we need to learn to play as hard as we work.

Leisure time is very important for high achievers. They generally operate at a high energy level and are very competitive, so they should try to develop hobbies and take part in sports and other activities that will be challenging as well as fun. No matter what your age or physical condition there are many hobby and sports activities that will help give you meaningful leisure time. The point is—do it! Remember: *All work and no play will probably lead to burnout someday!*

MAKE YOUR RELATIONSHIP WITH GOD YOUR TOP PRIORITY

It is impossible to have balance in life without a personal relationship with Jesus Christ. We are spiritual beings; if we leave God out of our lives, our lives will be out of balance.

Some "professional," full-time Christian leaders may be reading this book, along with other "nonprofessional" Christians. Therefore, I want to make clear the distinction between "religious activity" and a personal relationship with Jesus Christ. Many Christians are so involved with "religious activities" that their personal relationships with Jesus Christ suffer. It is possible to spend every day involved in various Christian activities and be so busy there is no time to spend with Christ.

One can burn out doing religious work just as easy as one can burn out working in business or other sorts of jobs. In fact, studies indicate that religious leaders are among the most susceptible to burnout. So when I say that you should make your relationship with God your top priority, I am not talking about filling your schedule up with more religious activities. I mean that getting to know God on a personal level and letting Him work His plan through you—instead of you trying to do it *for* Him—must become your top priority.

Samuel Stockton had pastored a church in New England for over twenty-five years when I met him during a seminar on burnout. Following the seminar I sat in the hotel lobby and listened to Pastor Stockton pour his heart out about his frustration with himself and his ministry.

"The bigger my church gets, the busier I get," he said. He explained that during the past five years the church had grown from two hundred people in a single Sunday morning worship service to over a thousand people all together in two morning worship services.

"I would like to think part of the reason they came was because of my good preaching," he said with a laugh. "But lately I can tell they are getting shortchanged. I've gotten so busy, I hardly have time to study for my sermons, and I hate to admit it, but there are lots of weeks I never have time to pray—except at mealtimes."

The difference between Pastor Stockton and a lot of other Christian leaders is that he was willing to admit that he hadn't been spending enough time with God. If we would spend more time with God, we would have more time for ourselves.

God wants all of us to live a balanced life. Jesus never got too busy to take time off for prayer. In Luke 5:15-16 we see how important Jesus' relationship with His Father was. "Now the report of His power spread even faster and vast crowds came to hear Him preach and to be healed of their diseases. But He often withdrew to the wilderness for prayer" (TLB). The busier Jesus got, the more time He spent with God. Notice that Scripture says He went off to the wilderness to pray. He could have prayed on His bed at night before He went to sleep. He could have gone to the synagogue to pray. He went to the wilderness so He could both relax and spend time with His Father.

Unfortunately, many Christian leaders react just the opposite to the way Jesus did. Like Samuel Stockton, the more their organizations grow and the busier they get, the less time they spend with God. As a result they try to get all the jobs done on their own strength instead of letting God accomplish the tasks through them.

Religious activity is not the same as spiritual maturity. The spiritually mature person makes sure there is time each day to get together with God for help, strength, and guidance. Failure to do so results in spiritual malnutrition, and spiritual malnutrition will ultimately cause physical and emotional exhaustion. We must never forget that it takes a balance of spiritual, physical, and emotional strength to accomplish things for God. We can't continue to give of ourselves physically, emotionally, and spiritually without being replenished, or we will burn ourselves out.

TWELVE

BLESSINGS OF BURNOUT

I dreaded this meeting. As I walked across the parking lot toward the restaurant, I thought to myself, *I'm going to tell him I'm not going to meet with him anymore!*

I was having another meeting with Jim Ander, who was helping me recover from burnout. He had given me an assignment to work on some long-range goals and for the second week in a row I didn't have my assignment completed. I was more than fifteen minutes late to this meeting. I had hoped he had gotten tired of waiting for me, but when I spotted his bright red Cadillac Eldorado in the parking lot, I knew he was still waiting for me.

After ordering a cup of coffee and a sweet roll, I started to offer another feeble excuse for why I was late and hadn't completed my assignments when Jim interrupted me by saying, "Myron, have you ever considered all the blessings you are receiving by going through burnout?"

I couldn't believe what I was hearing! At first I thought Jim was kidding, but then I realized he was serious and I got angry. Here I sat not even having enough emotional and physical energy to complete a simple assignment on time and feeling like life wasn't really worth the effort it took to get out of bed in the mornings, and my friend asks me a dumb question like that!

147

I sat speechless. I couldn't imagine a more stupid question! I wanted to get up and walk out of the restaurant, but I didn't because I didn't want to hurt my friend's feelings.

Jim saw the bewildered and frustrated look on my face. He smiled and said, "Myron, there are many great benefits of going through burnout. You have an opportunity many people never get."

For the next half hour or so I sat listening to Jim as he explained the many benefits and blessings associated with burnout. Even though I couldn't believe Jim at the time, as I look back, I can clearly see that everything he told me that morning was absolutely true. I can speak from experience that there are many benefits associated with going through burnout.

I want to pass on to you the things that Jim told me that day in the restaurant and that I later experienced for myself to be true. If you are going through burnout or know someone who is, take heart: *there are many wonderful blessings in burnout!*

THE IMPORTANCE OF THANKING GOD

That day in the restaurant I learned that as long as I continued to feel sorry for myself and had a negative attitude, I would never be able to discover the benefits of burnout. Jim reminded me of Romans 8:28: "And we know that in all things God works for the good of those who love Him, who have been called according to His purpose" (NIV). He also shared James 1:2-4 with me. "Dear brothers, is your life full of difficulties and temptations? Then be happy, for when the way is rough, your patience has a chance to grow. So let it grow, and don't try to squirm out of your problems. For when your patience is finally in full bloom, then you will be ready for anything, strong in character, full and complete" (TLB).

Even though I didn't feel like it, I made a decision that day to thank God in the midst of my burnout and to have a positive attitude about the situation, because according to James 1:2-4 God uses the difficulties and rough times in our lives to make us strong and complete people "ready for anything."

Even though I didn't have much faith in myself at that point, I was willing to believe God because I had learned from experience that God's Word is always true. I soon discovered that, true to God's Word, there were good things to be gained from my burnout. However, until I began believing Romans 8:28 and James 1:2-4 and stopped looking at the negatives, I couldn't see the positive side. The first step in discovering the blessings and benefits of burnout is to stop feeling sorry for yourself and being negative about your situation and to start applying Romans 8:28 and James 1:2-4 to your life.

ACCOMPLISHING GOD'S PURPOSE

God never calls us to burnout. He always calls us to bring glory to Him through a unique plan tailor-made for us. God's plan for us never included burnout.

We bring burnout on ourselves because we have never learned how to balance our lives and we have become caught in the trap of trying to do too much on our own without letting God work His plans through us using His power and resources.

In Psalm 50:15 God says, "I want you to trust Me in your times of trouble, so I can rescue you, and you can give Me glory" (TLB). God never intended for us to do it all by ourselves. God wants us to let Him work on our behalf so we can give Him the glory and credit rather than take it ourselves.

Going through burnout gives us the opportunity to learn that lesson. It also provides the opportunity to start accomplishing God's purpose for our lives instead of our own. Burnout is the result of getting off track, out of balance, and away from the will of God. All of us should be thankful for the opportunity to get back on track, balance our lives, and accomplish God's will, plan, and purpose for our lives.

STOPPING TO EVALUATE LIFE

Like the writer of the Book of Ecclesiastes, high achievers tend to get caught up in achieving things that don't really provide fulfillment in life. And that leads to burnout. Unfortunately, it sometimes takes an experience such as burnout for us to stop and realize that we are expending all of our physical and emotional energy on things that really don't produce what we expected them to.

I was so busy accomplishing my goals in life that I didn't take time to stop and really evaluate whether they were meeting my needs or accomplishing what God had planned for me. It took a burnout experience for God to get my attention so that I was willing to stop and evaluate my life. Had I not gone through burnout, I would still be plowing ahead, wearing myself out, going from goal to goal, but still without balance in my life.

Therefore, I can truly thank God for burnout. It provided an opportunity to evaluate what was really happening in my life—an opportunity many high achievers miss.

A FRESH START

This is a very exciting blessing! Many people go through their entire lives and never have a chance for a fresh start. It is very exciting to be able to have a new start in life with the tools necessary to keep life in balance.

During burnout we can learn a great deal about ourselves. We discover our limitations and our need to pace ourselves. We learn to slow down and experience life daily. We learn to put God back in the driver's seat of our lives. And coming out of burnout, we have the fantastic opportunity of putting all of these new-found tools into practice!

GREATER PRODUCTIVITY

When our lives are out of balance, we may be highly productive in one area of life but very unproductive in the other areas. As we recover from burnout, we learn how to have balance in life. Therefore, we are able to be productive in all areas of life, not just one or two.

This is a very rewarding experience. It broadens our interests and helps us become more complete persons—and that is exactly what James 1:2-4 promises! Let's look again at that passage.

> Dear brothers, is your life full of difficulties and temptations? Then be happy, for when the way is rough, your patience has a chance to grow. So let it grow, and don't try to squirm out of your problems. For when your patience is finally in full bloom, then you will be ready for anything, strong in character, full and complete (TLB).

What a great passage for the person in burnout! I can certainly identify with what it is teaching. There are tremendous blessings awaiting the person who goes through the difficulties and temptations associated with burnout. You can come out of the experience a full and complete person with balance in your life and ready for anything!

A NEW BASIS FOR A HEALTHY SELF-IMAGE

Many high achievers derive their self-images and self-esteem from their accomplishments. This is tragic, because when their productivity drops, their self-images suffer.

Building one's self-image on accomplishments makes it very hard to ever really learn the meaning of *grace* as taught in the Bible. God doesn't love us for what we do, He loves us in spite of what we do. Burnout gives us the opportunity to learn that very important lesson. We have the chance to discover that value to God has nothing to do with level of performance. When we discover that, we can have healthy self-images regardless of our productivity levels.

I can speak from experience that it is a great relief to learn that God's view of me has nothing to do with my ability to produce. I thank God for burnout, because I probably would never have gotten that very important insight into self-image had I not gone through it.

APPRECIATING GOD'S LOVE

God never gives up on a burnout victim, even though people in burnout are often ready to give up on life. I must confess I didn't really learn how much God loved me until I went through burnout. I discovered that God loves me even when I am unloving and unlovable in the eyes of other people.

I also discovered that even when your friends and family forsake you, God never does. He was always there. Even when I got so angry at Him that I threw my Bible across the room, God was there, ready to help and comfort me as soon as I would let Him.

I feel that one of the greatest benefits I derived from burnout was learning the true meaning of God's love. It is not conditional. It isn't based on our love for Him. It never changes no matter what we do. I knew that in theory before I burned out. But I learned it by experience when I went through burnout.

Burnout has greatly improved my relationship with God. I truly consider Him my Heavenly Father today. I realize just how much I need Him and how little He needs what I have to offer—but He loves me just as much anyway!

HELPING OTHERS IN BURNOUT

Another great blessing of burnout is that you are now in a position to help others in burnout or other difficulties they may be experiencing. Notice what 2 Corinthians 1:3-4 says.

> What a wonderful God we have—He is the Father of our Lord Jesus Christ, the source of every mercy, and the one who so wonderfully comforts and strengthens us in our hardships and trials. And why does He do this? So that when others are troubled, needing our sympathy and encouragement, we can pass on to them this same help and comfort God has given us" (TLB).

God helps us during our difficult times in life so we can

comfort others by reassuring them that He will also help them. This is a great blessing of burnout. During the past two years I have been able to share with countless others how God faithfully brought me through my battle with burnout. If He will help me, He will help you too. When He does, 2 Corinthians 1:3-4 tells us we have an obligation to share that help with others who are hurting.

So if you are experiencing burnout or any of its symptoms, take heart. Be encouraged! I can speak from experience that the rewards and blessings will greatly outweigh the current pain and frustrations. Remember, God loves you—and so do I!